He Is There and He Is Not Silent

Other books by Francis A. Schaeffer:

He Is There
and
He Is Not Silent

Francis A. Schaeffer

16380

TYNDALE HOUSE PUBLISHERS

Wheaton, Illinois

Library of Congress Catalog Card Number 72-79830
ISBN 8423-1412-1 cloth; 8423-1413-X paper.

First printing, June 1972.

Printed in the United States of America

To the L'Abri staff—Members and Workers, past and present. And to all those everywhere who are bound up with L'Abri in a special "bundle of life."

Contents

Introduction

In one way, this is the book that should have been written immediately after *The God Who Is There*. Over the last few years my wife, Edith, and I have been carrying through a somewhat comprehensive program of books. This book is one of the basic pieces, and without it the structure has inevitably been incomplete. Let me explain why.

My first two books were *The God Who Is There* and *Escape from Reason*. Many people assumed—perhaps because it is shorter—that *Escape from Reason* is the "introduction" and *The God Who Is There* a development of it. In fact, the opposite is the truth. *The God Who Is There* was written first and lays the ground work, establishes the terminology, and sets out the basic thesis. This is something for which we have struggled and struggled at L'Abri —a Christianity which has balance, not only exegetically and intellectually, but also in the area of reality and beauty; an insistence that beginning with the Christian system as God has given it to men in the verbalized propositional revelation of the Bible one can move along and find that every area of life is touched by truth and a song. *Escape from Reason* works out this principle particularly in the philosophical area of Nature and Grace, and shows how modern culture has grown from polluted roots far back in the late middle ages.

After those two books, this one should have come. That would have been its logical place. The three make a unified base and without them the various applications in the later books are really three feet off the ground. This book deals with one of the most fundamental of all questions: how we know, and how we know we know. Unless our epistemology is right, everything is going to be wrong. That is why I say that this book goes with *The God Who Is There* —a link emphasized by its title. The infinite-personal God is there, but also he is not silent; that changes the whole world. Wittgenstein, in his *Tractatus*, can find only silence in the area of values and meaning. Bergman made the same point in his film *Silence*. This book challenges their pessimism. He is there. He is not silent.

On the base of these three books of mine, which constitute a conscious unity which I believe rests on the unity of Scripture itself, all the other books which have come and will come depend. They apply this unified Christian system to various areas. It should be noted that *The God Who Is There* has two appendices which deal with two specific problems, the middle-class church in the twentieth century, and the practice of truth in Christian work and evangelism. These are developed in the later books. *Death in the City* is exegetical, picking up the application of the earlier books to American and North European culture as it has turned away from what God has given us as a base.

Next came *Pollution and the Death of Man*, the Christian answer to the ecological dilemma, based on the same consistent system. *The Church at the End of the Twentieth Century* moves on into other areas of application— sociology and also ecclesiology. The two appendices to that book, *Adultery and Apostasy* and *The Mark of the Christian* (also published as a separate small book), pick up the theme touched on in the second appendix to *The God Who Is There:* they emphasize the balance to be struck between the practice of the purity of the visible Church and the love which ought to mark relationships between all true Christians, no matter what their differences over secondary matters. There is also a fuller, and practical, treatment of ecclesiology in *The Church Before the Watching World*.

It might be alleged that this is merely a new, arid scholasticism, applied in the areas of epistemology, ecclesiology, ecology, sociology etc. If it were, then it would be nothing but a tinkling cymbal. Three books, however, redress the balance. The last chapter of *Death in the City*, "The Universe and Two Chairs," is important here. Edith's book, *L'Abri*, is a vital element, and without it the other books lack their true unity and balance. It shows how acting upon the fact that the infinite personal God is really there has worked out in day-by-day practice in the community of *L'Abri*. *True Spirituality* is also crucial; it is a systematic treatment of the whole basis of Christian living in an open relationship with God, and then with ourselves and others.

From all of this it will be clear that *The God Who Is There*, *Escape from Reason* and this book form a unity. Indeed, they could have been one book divided into various sections, with some subjects, Ecology, for instance, treated as extended footnotes, developing a detail of the case in a specific area. In the total of all the books Edith's book *Hidden Art* has an important place as it carries these things into the practical and beautiful area of creativity in the Christian's life. A book on the first eleven chapters of Genesis, entitled *Genesis in Space and Time*, will soon follow along, giving an even greater exegetical base at the decisive point of beginnings. Taken together, all of these books represent a unified concept which was developed over a long time of study and a long time of experiential knowledge of the God who is there, and is now being worked out in various disciplines.

It will also be clear that this book, dealing as it does with a primary area, forms a vital part of our case in speaking historic Christianity into the twentieth century. He is there and is not a silent, nor far-off, God.

The
1 Metaphysical
Necessity

This book will deal with the philosophic necessity of God's being there and not being silent, in the areas of metaphysics, morals, and epistemology.

We should understand first of all that the three basic areas of philosophic thought are what they have always been. The first of them is in the area of metaphysics, of "being." This is the area of what is—the problem of existence. This includes the existence of man, but we must realize that the existence of man is no greater problem as such than is the fact that anything exists at all. No one has said it better than Jean Paul Sartre, who has said that the basic philosophic question is that something is there rather than that nothing is there. Nothing that is worth calling a philosophy can sidestep the question of the fact that things do exist and that they exist in their present form and complexity. This is what we define, then, as the problem of metaphysics, the existence of being.

The second area of philosophical thought is that of man and the dilemma of man. Man is personal and yet he is finite, and so he is not a sufficient integration point for himself. We might remember another profound statement from Sartre, that no finite point has any meaning unless it has an infinite reference point. The Christian would agree that he is right in this statement.

Man is finite, so he is not a sufficient integration point for himself, yet man *is* different from non-man. Man is personal in contrast to that which is impersonal, or, to use a phrase which I have used in my books, man has his "mannishness."

Now behaviorism, and all forms of determinism, would say that man is not personal—that he is not intrinsically different from the impersonal. But the difficulty with this is that it denies the observation man has made of himself for 40,000 years, if we accept the modern dating system; and second, there is no determinist or behaviorist who really lives consistently on the basis of his determinism or his behavioristic psychology—saying, that is, that man is only a machine. This is true of Francis Crick, who reduces man to the mere chemical and physical properties of the DNA template. The interesting thing, however, is that Crick clearly shows that he cannot live with his own determinism. In one of his books, *Of Molecules and Men*, he soon begins to speak of nature as "her," and in a smaller, more profound book, *The Origin of the Genetic Code*, he begins to spell nature with a capital N. B. F. Skinner, author of *Beyond Freedom and Dignity*, shows the same tension. So there are these two difficulties with the acceptance of modern determinism and behaviorism, which say there is no intrinsic difference between man and non-man: first, one has to deny man's own observation of himself through all the years, back to the cave paintings and beyond; and second, no chemical determinist or psychological determinist is ever able to live as though he is the same as non-man.

Another question in the dilemma of man is man's nobility. Perhaps you do not like the word "nobility," but whatever word you choose, there is something great about man. I want to add here that evangelicals have made a horrible mistake by often equating the fact that man is lost and under God's judgment with the idea that man is nothing—a zero. This is not what the Bible says. There is something great about man, and we have lost perhaps our greatest opportunity of evangelism in our generation by not insisting that it is the Bible which explains *why* man is great.

However, man is not only noble (or whatever word you want to substitute), but man is also cruel. So we have a dilemma. The first dilemma is that man is finite and yet he is personal; the second dilemma is the contrast between man's nobility and man's cruelty. Or one can express it in a modern way: the alienation of man from himself and from all other men in the area of morals. So now we have two areas of philosophic thought: first, metaphysics, dealing with being, with existence; second, the area of morals.

The third area of this study is that of epistemology—the problem of knowing.

Now let me make two general observations. First, philosophy and religion deal with the same basic questions. Christians, and especially evangelical Christians, have tended to forget this. Philosophy and religion do not deal with different questions, though they give different answers and in different terms. The basic questions of both philosophy and religion (and I mean religion here in the wide sense, including Christianity) are the questions of being—that is, what exists; man and his dilemma—that is, morals; and of how man knows. Philosophy deals with these points, but so does religion, including evangelical, orthodox Christianity.

The second general observation concerns the two meanings of the word "philosophy," which must be kept absolutely separate if we are to avoid confusion. The first meaning is a discipline, an academic subject. That is what we usually think of as philosophy: a highly technical study which few people pursue. In this sense, few people are philosophers. But there is a second meaning that we must not miss if we are going to understand the problem of preaching the gospel in the twentieth-century world. For philosophy also means a man's *world view*. In this sense, all men are philosophers, for all men have a world view. This is just as true of the man digging a ditch as it is of the philosopher in the university.

Christians have tended to despise the concept of philosophy. This has been one of the weaknesses of evangelical, orthodox Christianity—we have been proud in despising philosophy, and we have been exceedingly proud in despising the intellectual. Our theological seminaries hardly ever relate their theology to philosophy, and specifically to the current philosophy. Thus, men go out from the theological seminaries not knowing how to relate it. It is not that they not know the answers, but my observation is that most men graduating from our theological seminaries do not know the questions.

In fact, philosophy is universal in scope. No man can live without a world view; therefore, there is no man who is not a philosopher.

There are not many possibilities in answer to the three basic areas of philosophic thought, but there is a great deal of possible detail surrounding the basic answers. It will help us tremendously—whether we are studying philosophy at university and feel buffeted to death, or whether we are trying to be ministers of the gospel, speaking to people with a world view—if we realize that although there are many possible details, the possible answers—in their basic concepts—are exceedingly few. There are two classes of answers given to these questions.

1. The first class of answer is that there is no logical, rational answer. This is rather a phenomenon of our own generation. The question has come under "the line of despair." I am not saying that nobody in the past had these views, but they were not the dominant view. Today it is much more dominant than it has ever been. This is true not only among philosophers in their discussions, but it is equally true of discussions on the street corner, at the cafe, at the university dining room, or at the filling station. The solution commonly proposed is that there is no logical, rational answer—all is finally chaotic, irrational, and absurd. This view is expressed with great finesse in the existential world of thinking, and in the theater of the absurd. This is the philosophy, or world view, of many people today. It is a part of the warp and woof of the thinking of our day, that there are no answers, that everything is irrational and absurd.

If a man held that everything is meaningless, nothing has answers and there is no cause-and-effect relationship, and if he really held this position with any consistency, it would be very hard to refute. But in fact, no one can hold consistently that everything is chaotic and irrational and that there are no basic answers. It can be held theoretically, but it cannot be held in practice that everything is absolute chaos.

The first reason the irrational position cannot be held consistently in practice is the fact that the external world is there and it has form and order. It is not a chaotic world. If it were true that all is chaotic, unrelated, and absurd, science as well as general life would come to an end. To live at all is not possible except in the understanding that the universe that is there—the external universe—has a certain form, a certain order, and that man conforms to that order and so he can live within it.

Perhaps you remember one of Godard's movies, *Pierrot le Fou*, in which he has people going out through the windows, instead of through the doors. But the interesting thing is that they do not go out through the solid wall. Godard is really saying that although he has no answer, yet at the same time he cannot go out through that solid wall. This is merely his expression of the difficulty of holding that there is a totally chaotic universe while the external world has form and order.

Sometimes people try to bring in a little bit of order; but as soon as you bring in a little bit of order, the first class of answer—that everything is meaningless, everything is irrational—is no longer self-consistent, and falls to the ground.

The view that everything is chaotic and there are no ultimate answers is held by many thinking people today, but in my experience they always hold it very selectively. Almost without exception (actually, I have never found an exception), they discuss rationally until they are losing the discussion and then they try to slip over into the answer of irrationality. But as soon as the one we are discussing with does that, we must point out to him that as soon as he becomes selective in his argument of irrationality, he makes his whole argument suspect. Theoretically the position of irrationalism can be held, but no one lives with it in regard either to the external world or the categories of his thought world and discussion. As a matter of fact, if this position were argued properly, all discussion would come to an end. Communication would end. We would have only a series of meaningless sounds—blah, blah, blah. The theater of the absurd has said this, but it fails, because if you read and listen carefully to the theater of the absurd, it is always trying to communicate its view that one cannot communicate. There is always a communication about the statement that there is no communication. It is always selective, with pockets of order brought in somewhere along the line. Thus we see that this class of answer—that all things are irrational—is not an answer.

2. The second class of answer is that there is an answer which can be rationally and logically considered, which can be communicated to oneself in one's thought world, and communicated with others externally. In this chapter we will deal with metaphysics in the area of answers that can be discussed; later we will deal with man in his dilemma, the area of morals, in relation to answers that can be discussed. So now we are to consider such answers in the area of being, of existence.

I have already said that there are not many basic answers, although there are variances of details within the answers. Now curiously enough, there are only three possible basic answers to this question which would be open to rational consideration. The basic answers are very, very few indeed.

We are considering existence, the fact that something is there. Remember Jean Paul Sartre's statement that the basic philosophic question is that something is there rather than that nothing is there. The first basic answer is that everything that exists has come out of absolutely nothing. In other words, you begin with nothing. Now, to hold this view, it must be *absolutely* nothing. It must be what I call *nothing* nothing. It cannot be nothing something or something nothing. If one is going to accept this answer, it must be nothing nothing, which means there must be no energy, no mass, no motion, and no personality.

My description of nothing nothing runs like this. Suppose we had a very black blackboard which had never been used. On this blackboard we drew a circle and inside that circle there was everything that was—and there was nothing within the circle. Then we erase the circle. This is nothing nothing. You must not let anybody say he is giving an answer beginning with nothing and then really begin with something: energy, mass, motion, or personality. That would be something, and something is not nothing.

The truth is I have never heard this argument sustained, for it is unthinkable that all that now is has come out of utter nothing. But theoretically, that is the first possible answer.

The second possible answer in the area of existence is that all that now is had an impersonal beginning. This impersonality may be mass, energy, or motion, but they are all impersonal, and all equally impersonal. So it makes no basic philosophic difference which of them you begin with. Many modern men have implied that because they are beginning with energy particles rather than old-fashioned mass, they have a better answer. Salvador Dali did this as he moved from his surrealistic period into his new mysticism. But such men do not have a better answer. It is still impersonal. Energy is just as impersonal as mass or motion. As soon as you accept the impersonal beginning of all things, you are faced with some form of reductionism. Reductionism argues that everything there is now, from the stars to man himself, is finally to be understood by reducing it to the original, impersonal factor or factors.

The great problem with beginning with the impersonal is to find any meaning for the particulars. A particular is any individual factor, any individual thing—the separate parts of the whole. A drop of water is a particular, and so is a man. If we begin with the impersonal, then how do any of the particulars that now exist—including man— have any meaning, any significance? Nobody has given us an answer to that. In all the history of philosophical thought, whether from the East or the West, no one has given us an answer.

Beginning with the impersonal, everything, including man, must be explained in terms of the impersonal plus time plus chance. Do not let anyone divert your mind at this point. There are no other factors in the formula, because there are no other factors that exist. If we begin with an impersonal, we cannot then have some form of teleological concept. No one has ever demonstrated how time plus chance, beginning with an impersonal, can produce the needed complexity of the universe, let alone the personality of man. No one has given us a clue to this.

Often this answer—of beginning with the impersonal —is called pantheism. The new mystical thought in the underground newspapers is almost always some form of pantheism—and almost all the modern liberal theology is pantheistic as well. Often this beginning with the impersonal is *called* pantheism, but really this is a semantic trick, because by using the root "theism," a connotation of the personal is brought in, when by definition the impersonal is meant. In my discussions I never let anybody talk unthinkingly about pantheism. Somewhere along the way I try to make the point that it is not really pan*theism*, with its semantic illusion of personality, but pan*everythingism*. The ancient religions of Hinduism and Buddhism, as well as of the modern mysticism, the new "pantheistic" theology, are not truly pan*theism*. It is merely a semantic solution which is being offered. "Theism" is being used as a connotation word. In *The God Who Is There** I have emphasized the fact that the modern solutions are usually semantic mysticisms, and this is one of them.

But whatever form paneverythingism takes, including the modern scientific form which reduces everything to

---

*Inter-Varsity Press, Downers Grove, Illinois.

energy particles, it always has the same problem: in all of them, the end is the impersonal.

There are two problems which always exist—the need for unity and the need for diversity. Paneverythingism gives an answer for the need of unity, but it gives none for the needed diversity. Beginning with the impersonal, there is no meaning or significance to diversity. We can think of the old Hindu pantheism, which begins everything with *om*. In reality, everything ought to have ended with *om* on a single note, with no variance, because there is no reason for significance in variance. And even if paneverythingism gave an answer for form, it gives no meaning for freedom. Cycles are usually introduced as though waves were being tossed up out of the sea, but this gives no final solution to any of these problems. Morals, under every form of pantheism, have no meaning as morals, for everything in paneverythingism is finally equal. Modern theology must move towards situational ethics because there is no such thing as morals in this cycle. The word "morals" is used, but it is really only a word. This is the dilemma of the second answer, which is the one that most hold today. Naturalistic science holds it, beginning everything with energy particles. Many university students hold some form of paneverythingism. Liberal theological books today are almost uniformly pantheist. But beginning with an impersonal, as the pantheist must do, there are no true answers in regard to existence with its complexity, or the personality—the mannishness—of man.[1]

The third possible answer is to begin with a personal beginning. With this we have exhausted the possible basic answers in regard to existence. It may sound simplistic, but it is true. That is not to say there are no details that one can discuss, no variances, subheadings, or subschools—but these are the only basic schools of thought which are possible. Somebody once brilliantly said that when you get done with any basic question there are not many people in the room. By this he meant that the farther you go in depth in any basic question, finally the choices to be made are rather simple and clear. There are not many basic answers to any of the great questions of life.

So now let us think what it means to begin with that which is personal. That is, that which is personal began everything else, the very opposite of beginning with the impersonal. In this case man, being personal, does h because it is not alienated from what has always been, and what is, and what always will be. This is our answer, and with this we have a solution not only to the problem of existence—of bare being and its complexity—but also for man's being different, with a personality which distinguishes him from non-man.

We may use an illustration of two valleys. Often in the Swiss Alps there is a valley filled with water and an adjacent valley without water. Surprisingly enough, sometimes the mountain spring leaks, and suddenly the second derstood that you have to have absolutes, or nothing has meaning. But the difficulty facing Plato was the fact that his gods were not big enough to meet the need. So although he knew the need, the need fell to the ground because his gods were not big enough to be the point of reference or place of residence for his absolutes, for his ideals. In Greek literature the Fates sometimes seem to be behind and controlling the gods, and sometimes the gods seem to be controlling the Fates. Why the confusion? Because everything fails in their thinking at this point—because their limited gods are not big enough. That is why we need a personal-infinite God. That is first.

Second, we need a personal unity and diversity in God —not just an abstract concept of unity and diversity, because we have seen we need a personal God. We need a personal unity and diversity. Without this we have no answer.

What we are talking about is the philosophic necessity, in the area of being and existence, of the fact that God is there. That is what it is all about: *He is there.*

There is no other sufficient philosophical answer than the one I have outlined. You can search through university philosophy, underground philosophy, filling station philosophy—it does not matter which—there is no other sufficient philosophical answer to existence, to being, than the one I have outlined. There is only one philosophy, one religion, that fills this need in all the world's thought, whether the East, the West, the ancient, the modern, the new, the old. Only one fills the philosophical need of existence, of being, and it is the Judaeo-Christian God—not just an abstract concept, but rather that this God is really there. He really exists. There is no other answer, and orthodox Christians ought to be ashamed of having been defensive for so long. It is not a time to be defensive. There is no other answer.

Let us notice that no word is as meaningless as is the

word "god." Of itself it means nothing. Like any other word, it is only a linguistic symbol—g-o-d—until content is put into it. This is especially so for the word "god," because no other word has been used to convey such absolutely opposite meanings. The mere use of the word "god" proves nothing. You must put content into it. The word "god" as such is no answer to the philosophic problem of existence, but the Judaeo-Christian content to the word "God" as given in the Old and New Testaments does meet the need of what exists—the existence of the universe in its complexity and of man as man. And what is that content? It relates to an infinite-personal God, who is personal unity in diversity on the high order of trinity.

Every once in a while in my discussions someone asks how I can believe in the Trinity. My answer is always the same. I would still be an agnostic if there were no Trinity, because there would be no answers. Without the high order of personal unity and diversity as given in the Trinity, *there are no answers.*

Let us return again to the personal-infinite. On the side of God's infinity, there is a complete chasm between God on one side and man, the animal, the flower, and the machine on the other. On the side of God's infinity, he stands alone. He is the absolute other. He is, in his infinity, contrary to all else. He is differentiated from all else because only he is infinite. He is the Creator; all else was created. He is infinite; all else is finite. All else is brought forth by creation, so all else is dependent and only he is independent. This is absolute on the side of his infinity. Therefore, concerning God's infinity, man is as separated from God as is the atom or any other machine-portion of the universe.

But on the side of God being personal, the chasm is between man and the animal, the plant, and the machine. Why? Because man was made in the image of God. This is not just "doctrine." It is not dogma that needs just to be repeated linearly, as McLuhan would say. This is really down in the warp and woof of the whole problem. Man is made in the image of God; therefore, on the side of the fact that God is a personal God the chasm stands not between God and man, but between man and all else. But on the side of God's infinity, man is as separated from God as the atom or any other finite of the universe. So we have the answer to man's being finite and yet personal.

It is not that this is the best answer to existence; it is the *only* answer. That is why we may hold our Christianity with intellectual integrity. The only answer for what exists is that he, the infinite-personal God, really is there.

Now we must develop the second part a bit farther—personal unity and diversity on the high order of trinity. Einstein taught that the whole material world may be reduced to electromagnetism and gravity. At the end of his life he was seeking a unity above these two, something that would unite electromagnetism and gravity, but he never found it. But what if he had found it? It would only be unity in diversity in relationship to the material world, and as such it would only be child's play. Nothing would really have been settled because the needed unity and diversity in regard to personality would not have been touched. If he had been able to bring electromagnetism and gravity together, he would not have explained the need of personal unity and diversity.

In contrast, let us think of the Nicene Creed—three Persons, one God. Rejoice that they chose the word "person." Whether you realize it or not, that catapulted the Nicene Creed right into our century and its discussions: three Persons in existence, loving each other, and in communication with each other, before all else was.

If this were not so, we would have had a God who needed to create in order to love and communicate. In such a case, God would have needed the universe as much as the universe needed God. But God did not need to create; God does not need the universe as the universe needs him. Why? Because we have a full and true Trinity. The Persons of the Trinity communicated with each other, and loved each other before the creation of the world.

This is not only an answer to the acute philosophic need of unity in diversity, but of *personal* unity and diversity. The unity and diversity cannot exist before God or be behind God, because whatever is farthest back *is* God. But with the doctrine of the Trinity, unity and diversity is God himself—three Persons, yet one God. That is what the Trinity is, and nothing less than this.

We must appreciate that our Christian forefathers understood this very well in A.D. 325, when they stressed the three Persons in the Trinity, as the Bible had clearly set this forth. Let us notice that it is not that they invented the Trinity in order to give an answer to the philosophical questions which the Greeks of that time understood very dynamically. It is quite the contrary. The unity and diversity problem was there, and they realized that in the Trinity as it had been taught in the Bible they had an answer that no one else had. They did not invent the Trinity to meet the need; the Trinity was already there and it *met* the need. They realized that in the Trinity we have what all these people are arguing about and defining but for which they have no answer.

Let us notice again that this is not the *best* answer; it is the *only* answer. Nobody else, no philosophy, has ever given us an answer for unity and diversity. So when people ask whether we are embarrassed intellectually by the Trinity, I always switch it over into their own terminology—unity and diversity. Every philosophy has this problem and no philosophy has an answer. Christianity does have an answer in the existence of the Trinity. The only answer to what exists is that he, the triune God, is there.

So we have said two things. The only answer to the metaphysical problem of existence is that the infinite-personal God is there; and the only answer to the metaphysical problem of existence is that he, the Trinity, is there—the triune God.

Now surely by this time we will have become convinced that philosophy and religion are indeed dealing with the same questions. Notice that in the basic concept of existence, of being, it is the Christian answer or nothing. It will change your life if you understand this, no matter how evangelical and orthodox you are.

Let me add something, in passing. I find that many people who are evangelical and orthodox want truth just to be true to the dogmas, or to be true to what the Bible says. Nobody stands more for the full inspiration of Scripture than I, but this is not the end of truth as Christianity is presented, as the Bible presents itself. *The truth of Christianity is that it is true to what is there.* You can go to the end of the world and you never need be afraid, like the ancients, that you will fall off the end and the dragons will eat you up. You can carry out your intellectual discussion to the end of the game, because Christianity is not only true to the dogmas, it is not only true to what God has said in the Bible, but it is also true to what is there, and you will never fall off the end of the world! It is not just an approximate model; it really is true to what is there. When the evangelical catches that—when evangelicalism catches that—we may have our revolution. We will begin to have something beautiful and alive, something which will have force in our poor, lost world. This is what truth is from the Christian viewpoint and as God sets it forth in the Scripture. But if we are going to have this answer, notice that we must have the *full biblical* answer, and not reduce

Christianity to either the paneverythingism of the East, or the paneverythingism of modern, liberal theology, whether Protestant or Roman Catholic. We *must not* allow a theological pantheism to begin to creep in, and we must not reduce Christianity to the modern existential, upper-story theology. If we are going to have these great, titanic answers, Christianity must be the full biblical answer. We need the full biblical position to have the answer to the basic philosophical problem of the existence of what is. We need the full biblical content concerning God: that he is the infinite-personal God, and the triune God.

Now let me express this in a couple of other ways. One way to say it is that without the infinite-personal God, the God of personal unity and diversity, there is no answer to the existence of what exists. We can say it in another way, however, and that is that the infinite-personal God, the God who is Trinity, has spoken. He is there, and he is not silent. There is no use having a silent God. We would not know anything about him. He has spoken and told us what he is and that he existed before all else, and so we have the answer to the existence of what is.

He is not silent. The reason we have the answer is because the infinite-personal God, the full trinitarian God, has not been silent. He has told us who he is. Couch your concept of inspiration and revelation in these terms, and you will see how it cuts down into the warp and woof of modern thinking. *He is not silent.* That is the reason we know. It is because he has spoken. What has he told us? Has he told us only about other things? No, he has told us true truth about himself—and because he has told us true truth about himself—that he is the infinite-personal, triune God—we have the answer to existence. Or we may put it this way: at the point of metaphysics—of being, of existence—general and special revelation speak with one voice. All these ways of saying it are really expressing the same thing from slightly different viewpoints.

In conclusion, man, beginning with himself, can define the philosophical problem of existence, but he cannot generate from himself the answer to the problem. The answer to the problem of existence is that the infinite-personal, triune God is there, and that the infinite-personal, triune God is not silent.

------

[1]Some might say there is another possibility—some form of dualism, that is, two opposites existing simultaneously as co-equal and co-eternal. For example, mind (or ideals or ideas) and matter; or in morals, good and evil. However, if in morals one holds this position, then there is no ultimate reason to call one good and one evil—the words and choice are purely subjective if there is not something above them. And if there is something above them it is no longer a true dualism. In metaphysics, the dilemma is that no one finally rests with dualism. Back of Yin and Yang there is placed a shadowy Tao; back of Zoroastrianism there is placed an intangible thing or figure. The simple fact is that in any form of dualism we are left with some form of imbalance or tension and there is a motion back to a monism.

Either men try to find a unity over the two; or in the case of the concept of a parallelism (for example, ideals or ideas and material) there is a need to find a relationship, a correlation or contact between the two, or we are left with a concept of the two keeping step with no unity to cause them to do so. Thus in an attempted parallelism there has been a constant tendency for one side to be subordinated to the other, or for one side to become an illusion.

Further, if the elements of the dualism are impersonal, we are left with the same problem in both being and morals as in the case of a more simple form of a final impersonal. Thus, for me, dualism is not the same kind of basic answer as the three I deal with in this book.

Perhaps it would be well to point out that in both existence and morals, Christianity gives a unique and sufficient answer in regard to a present dualism yet original monism. In existence, God is spirit—this is as true of the Father as of the Holy Spirit, and equally true of the Son, prior to the incarnation. Thus, we begin with a monism, but with a creation by the infinite God of the material universe out of nothing, a dualism now exists. It should be noted that while God thus created something which did not exist before, it is not a beginning out of nothing nothing, because he was there (as the infinite-personal God) to will.

The
2 Moral
Necessity

We now turn to the second area of philosophic thought, which is man and the dilemma of man. There are, as we have seen, two problems concerning man and his dilemma. The first of them is the fact that man is personal, different from non-man, and yet finite. Because he is finite, he has no sufficient integration point in himself. Again, as Jean Paul Sartre put it, if a finite point does not have an infinite reference point, it is meaningless and absurd.

Yet despite this, man is different from non-man; he is personal; he has the mannishness of man which distinguishes him from non-man. This is the first problem: he is different because of his mannishness and yet he is finite. He does not have a sufficient integration point within himself.

The second point concerning man and the dilemma of man is what I call the nobility of man. We might not like this term, because of its romantic ties with the past, but still there is the wonder of man—but contrasted with this there is his cruelty. So man stands with all his wonder and nobility, and yet also with his horrible cruelty that runs throughout the warp and woof of man's history.

Or we could express it in yet another way—man's estrangement from himself and other men in the area of morals. And this brings us to the word "morals." Up to this point we have concerned ourselves with the problem of metaphysics, but now we enter the area of morals.

Leaving aside the "answer" that says there are no answers in the area of reason, the first answer given to this dilemma of morals is (as in the area of metaphysics) the impersonal beginning. As we consider man's finiteness and his cruelty, it would certainly seem that these things are not one, but two. Mankind has always thought of these things as being different. Man's finiteness is his smallness; he is not a sufficient reference point to himself. But his cruelty has always been considered as distinct from his finiteness. Yet we must notice something. If we accept the impersonal beginning, finally we will come to the place where man's finiteness and his cruelty become the same thing. This is an absolute rule. No matter what kind of impersonality we begin with, whether it is the modern scientist with his energy particles, or the paneverythingism of the East, or neo-orthodox theology, eventually these two things merge into one problem rather than two. With an impersonal beginning, morals really do not exist as morals. If one starts with an impersonal beginning, the answer to morals eventually turns out to be the assertion that there are no morals (in however sophisticated a way this may be expressed). This is true whether one begins with the Eastern pantheism or the new theology's pantheism, or with the energy particle. With an impersonal beginning, everything is finally equal in the area of morals. With an impersonal beginning, eventually morals is just another form of metaphysics, of being. Morals disappear and there is only one philosophic area rather than two.

Left in this position, we can talk about what is antisocial, or what society does not like, or even what I do not like, but we cannot talk about what is really right and what is really wrong. If we begin with the impersonal, man's alienation as he is now is only because of chance; he has become that which is out of line with what the universe has always been, that is, the impersonal. So man's dilemma, man's tension, is never on the moral side, if you begin with the impersonal; but rather, if you extend the argument far enough, man has been kicked out of line with the universe as it always has been and is intrinsically.

Assuming the beginning was impersonal, man has, by chance, become a being with aspirations, including moral motions for which there is no ultimate fulfillment in the universe as it is. Man has been "kicked up" in the way that he has developed a feeling of moral motions, when in reality these have no meaning in the universe as it is. Here is the ultimate cosmic alienation, the dilemma of our generation—Giacometti, with his figures standing there always alienated from everybody else and from the spectator as he observes them in the museum. The problem of our generation is a feeling of cosmic alienation, including the area of morals. Man has a feeling of moral motions, yet in the universe as it is, it is completely out of line with what is there.

You may ask why I use the term "moral motions." I choose the term simply because I am not talking about specific norms. I am talking about the fact that men have always felt that things are right and things are wrong. I am not talking about certain norms being right or wrong. All men have this sense of moral motions. You do not find man without them anywhere back in antiquity. You do not find the little girl prostitute upon the street without some feeling of moral motions. You do not find the determinist, the behaviorist in psychology, without the feeling of moral motions, even if he says morals as morals do not exist. So we find man cast up with a feeling of moral motions which in reality leads only to a complete cosmic alienation, because if you begin with the impersonal, in the universe as it is there is no place for morals as morals. There is no standard in the universe which gives final meaning to such words as right and wrong. If you begin with the impersonal, the universe is totally silent concerning any such words.

Thus, to the pantheist, the final wrong or tension is the failure to accept your impersonality. If you look to those places in the East where pantheism has worked itself out more consistently than in our modern, liberal theology or the hippie-type of pantheism, you will find that the final wrong in man, the final Karma, if you will, is the fact that he will not accept his impersonality. In other words, he will not accept who he is.

In the Hindu paneverythingism there is a high development of the fact that there is no ultimate difference between cruelty and non-cruelty. This can be seen clearly in the person of Kali. In all the Hindu representations of God, there is always a feminine figure. Sometimes people say there is a trinity in Hinduism because there are three different faces shown in a bas-relief. But this is only because they do not understand that it is only a bas-relief. There are really five faces in a Hindu presentation—four around, if you have a free-standing figure, and one on top, looking upward, even if you cannot see it or even if it is not actually carved. There is no trinity in Hinduism. Not only is it not three but five, but even more important, these are not persons, they are only manifestations of the final, impersonal god. But one of the manifestations is always feminine, because the feminine must be there as well as the masculine. But interestingly enough, the feminine Kali is also always the destroyer. She is often pictured as having great fangs, with skulls hanging around her neck. Why? Because finally, cruelty is just as much a part of what is as is non-cruelty. So you have Vishnu taking his three constructive steps, but on the other hand you must always see Kali, the one who tears down, the one who destroys, the one who is ready to devour your flesh and tear you to pieces. Cruelty is as much a part of all that is, as is non-cruelty.

Why is the cruel part always feminine? Nobody knows, but I would hazard a guess that it is a perverted memory concerning Eve. Myth usually says something—it goes back to something—but it has also usually become perverted.

But eventually, as you examine the new theology as well as the pantheism of the East, you come to the place where you cannot rightly speak of right or wrong. In Western religious paneverythingism, we find men trying to stem off this situation, and to retain a distinction between cruelty and non-cruelty. They try to hold off the arrival at the place where they have to acknowledge that there is no basic meaning to the words "right" and "wrong." But it cannot be done. It is like starting a stone downhill. Beginning with the impersonal, though one may use religious terms and even Christian terms, there is no final absolute and there are no final categories concerning right and wrong. Hence, what is left may be worded in many different ways in different cultures, but it is only the relative—that which is sociological, statistical, situational—nothing else. You have situational, statistical ethics—the standard of averages—but you cannot have morality.

Finally, we must understand that in this setting, to be right is just as meaningless as to be wrong. Morals as morals disappear and what we are left with is just metaphysics. We are just the little against the big, and nothing that has meaning in right and wrong.

We are rapidly coming to this in our modern culture. Consider Marshall McLuhan's concept that democracy is finished. What will we have in place of democracy or morals? He says there is coming a time in the global village (not far ahead, in the area of electronics) when we will be able to wire everybody up to a giant computer, and what the computer strikes as the average at a given moment will be what is right and wrong. You may say that is far-fetched; not so, because you must understand that that is exactly what Kinsey set forth as statistical sexual ethics. It is the way modern Sweden runs its sexual ethics. This is not theoretical. We have come to this place in our Western culture because man sees himself as beginning from the impersonal, the energy particle and nothing else. We are left with only statistical ethics, and in that setting, there is simply no such thing as morals.

If we use religious language instead of secular language, it may seem to remove the strain somewhat. But when we get behind the religious words, they have no more real meaning than the naturalistic, psychological reduction of morals to conditioning and reflexes. Behind the religious-connotation words, we find only the same problem as we find in the secular world. The concept of morals as morals eventually just disappears. The man who has expressed this better than anyone else is the Marquis de Sade, with his chemical determinism, who simply made this statement: "What is, is right." No one can argue against this, if we begin with an impersonal beginning.

Let us summarize: Beginning with the impersonal, there is no explanation for the complexity of the universe or the personality of man. As I said in the previous chapter, it is not that Christianity is a better answer, but that if you begin with the impersonal, in reality you do not have any answer at all to the metaphysical questions. And the same thing is true in the area of morals. If you begin with an impersonal, no matter how you phrase that impersonal, there is no meaning for morals.

Now let us look at the opposite answer—the personal beginning. In this answer, there is a possibility of keeping morals and metaphysics separate. This is a profound thing, though it may sound simple. Whereas the impersonal beginning leads us to a merging of morals and metaphysics, the personal beginning provides the possibility of keeping them separate. In other words, man's finiteness may be separated from his cruelty.

However, as soon as we say this we are faced with a tremendous question. If we begin with a personal beginning and look at man as he now is, how do we explain the dilemma of man's cruelty? In what perspective do we regard this?

There are two possibilities. The first is that man as he is now in his cruelty is what he has always *intrinsically* been: that is what man is. The symbol m-a-n equals that which is cruel, and the two cannot be separated. But if it is true that man has always been cruel, we are faced with two problems.

I want to deal with the first of these at length. If man was created by a personal-infinite God, how can we escape the conclusion that the personal God who made man cruel is himself also bad and cruel? This is where the French thinkers Charles Baudelaire and Albert Camus come on the scene. Baudelaire, who was a famous art historian and a great thinker, has a famous sentence: "If there is a God, he is the Devil." At first, Bible-believing Christians may react negatively to this sentence. But after thought, a real Christian would agree with Baudelaire that if there is an unbroken line between what man is now and what he has always intrinsically been, then if there is a God, he is the Devil. Although as Christians, we would definitely differ from Baudelaire, we would agree with this conclusion *if* we begin with his premise.

Now Camus dealt with the same problem from a slightly different viewpoint. He argued that if there is a God, then we cannot fight social evil, for if we do, we are fighting God who made the world as it is. What these two men say is, I think, irrefutable if we accept the basic premise that man stands where he has always stood—that there has been a continuity of intrinsic cruelty.

At this point, there are those who offer a selective answer in the area of irrationality. The first class of answer we dealt with in chapter one was the one which says there are no answers—everything is finally chaotic and irrational. Much that is religious, and specifically the Western liberal theology, moves over into the field of irrationality and says, "We have no answer for this, but let us take a step of faith against all reason and all reasonableness and say that God is good." That is the position of all modern liberal theology, whether it is the old-line rational liberalism or whether it is the Barthian thinking. But this should be seen for what it is: a part of the answer of chaos and irrationality.

I have said that people who argue irrationality to be the answer are always selective about where they will become irrational. That is certainly true of this area. Suddenly men who have been saying that they are arguing with great reason become irrationalists at this point, and say that there is only an irrational answer for the question of how God is good. Liberal modern theology is firmly fixed in this classification.

Let us look at this more carefully. As soon as irrationality is brought in at this point, it will lead to tension in two directions at the same time. First, there will be a motion back toward reason. As people argue that God is a good God against all reason and rationality, there is something in them that is in tension. Consequently, liberals who offer this answer frequently split off back into reason, and every time they do, they lose this blindly optimistic answer. As soon as they enter reason, the optimistic answer is gone, because all the optimism concerning God's goodness rests upon irrationality. If they step back into the area of reason, they are back into pessimism; that is, if there is a God he is a bad God. In Baudelaire's words, he is the Devil. As one flees into irrationality at this point, there is the tendency to spin off back into pessimism.

The other tension that is immediately set up when people give this answer is to spin off in the opposite direction, towards making everything irrational. As they spin off towards irrationality, they ask, where do I stop? They tend to say that perhaps one should just accept the whole irrational, chaotic situation, and decide that there is no meaning in the use of religious "god-words" at all. Irrationalism cannot be shut up to saying God is good against all reason. These are the two tensions that are set up as soon as one tries to bring in the answer of irrationality at this crucial point.

The second problem inherent in this situation is that if we say that man in his present cruelty is what man has always been, and what man intrinsically is, how can there be any hope of a qualitative change in man? There may be a quantitative change, that is, he may become just a little less cruel, but there can never be qualitative change. If God has made man as man now is then this is what man as man is. So we are left with pessimism in regard to man and his actions. These are the two problems that arise if one takes the position that man is made by a personal God, has a personal beginning rather than an impersonal beginning, and that man has always been what he now is.

Let us go back, however. Let us say that we are on the side of a personal beginning, that man has been made by that which is personal rather than merely being a part of a total, final, complete impersonal everything-there-is. We come back to a personal beginning for man, man created by a personal God. At this point we must recognize a second possibility, that man as he is now is not what he was; that man is discontinuous with what he has been, rather than continuous with what he has been. Or, to put it another way, man is now abnormal—he has changed.

This involves yet another question and choice: If God changed him, or made him abnormal, then he is still a bad God, and we have solved nothing. But there is another possibility: that man created by God as personal has changed *himself*—that he stands at the point of discontinuity rather than continuity not because God changed him but because he changed himself. Man as he now is by his own choice is not what he intrinsically was. In this case we can understand that man is now cruel, but that God is not a bad God. This is precisely the Judaeo-Christian position.

We have taken all the philosophical possibilities and we have seen what is wrong, and where they lead in each case. Now we have come to the other possibility, the Judaeo-Christian position. There was a space-time, historic change in man. There is a discontinuity and not a continuity in man. Man, made in the image of God and not programmed, turned by choice from his proper integration point at a certain time in history. When he did this, man became something that he previously was not, and the dilemma of man becomes a true moral problem rather than merely a metaphysical one. Man, at a certain point of history, changed himself, and hence stands, in his cruelty, in discontinuity with what he was, and we have a true moral situation: morals suddenly exist. Everything hangs upon the fact that man is abnormal now, in contrast to what he originally was.

The difference between Christian thinking and the non-Christian philosopher has always been at this point. The non-Christian philosopher has always said that man is normal now, but biblical Christianity says he is abnormal now. It is interesting in this regard that the later Heidegger saw that you could not come up with final answers if you said that man is always normal, and he in his own way says man is abnormal. But he proposed a very different kind of abnormality, an epistemological one, at the point of Aristotle. This does not give any real answer to the problem, but it is intriguing that Heidegger, perhaps the greatest of the modern non-Christian philosophers, did see that the position that man is normal leads to a dead end.

When you come to the Christian answer, however, that is, that man is abnormal now because at a point of space-time history he changed himself (not epistemologically but morally) four things immediately emerge.

1. We can now explain what is, namely, that man is now cruel, without God being a bad God.

2. There is a hope of a solution for this moral problem which is not intrinsic to the mannishness of man. If his cruelty is intrinsic to the mannishness of man—if that is what man always has been intrinsically, then there is no hope of a solution. But if it is an abnormality, there is a hope of a solution. It is in this setting that the substitutionary, propitiatory death of Christ ceases to be an incomprehensible concept. In liberal theology, the death of Christ is always an incomprehensible god-word. But in this setting to which we have come, the substitutionary death of Christ now has meaning. It is not merely god-words or an upper-story, existential thing. It has solid meaning. We can have the hope of a solution concerning man if man is abnormal now.

3. On this basis we can have a real ground for fighting evil, including social evil and social injustice.

Modern man has no real basis for fighting evil, because he sees man as normal—whether he comes out of the paneverythingism of the East or modern liberal theology, or out of the paneverythingism of everything's being reduced (including man) to only the energy particle. But the Christian has—he can fight evil without fighting God. He has the solution for Camus' problem: we can fight evil without fighting God, because God did not make things as they are now—as man in his cruelty has made them. God did not make man cruel, and he did not make the results of man's cruelty. These are abnormal, contrary to what God made, and so we can fight the evil *without fighting God*.

In another one of my books, I have used the account of Jesus before the tomb of Lazarus. To me, what Jesus did at the tomb of Lazarus sets the world on fire; it becomes a great shout into the morass of the twentieth century. Jesus came to the tomb of Lazarus. The One who claims to be God stood before the tomb, and the Greek language makes it very plain that he had two emotions. The first was tears for Lazarus; but the second emotion was blinding anger. He was furious; and he could be furious at the evil of death without being furious with himself as God. This is tremendous in the context of the twentieth century. When I look at evil—the abnormal cruelty which is not the thing as God made it—my reaction should be the same. I am able not only to cry for the evil, but I can be angry at the evil—as long as I am careful that egoism does not enter into my reaction. I have a basis to fight the thing which is abnormal to what God has made.

The Christian should be in the front line, fighting the results of man's cruelty, for we know that it is not what God has made. We are able to be angry at the results of man's cruelty without being angry at God or being angry at what is normal.

4. We can have real morals and moral absolutes, for

now God is absolutely good, with the total exclusion of evil from God. God's character is the moral absolute of the universe. Plato was entirely right when he held that unless you have absolutes morals do not exist. Here is the complete answer to Plato's dilemma; he spent his time trying to find a place to root his absolutes but he was never able to do so because his gods were not enough. But here is the infinite-personal God who has a character from which all evil is excluded, and so his character is the moral absolute of the universe.

It is not that there is a moral absolute *behind* God that binds man and God, because that which is farthest back is always finally God. Rather, it is God himself and his character which is the moral absolute of the universe.

Again, as in the area of metaphysics, we must understand that this is not simply the best answer—it is the only answer in morals for man in his dilemma. The only answer in the area of morals, as true morals, including the problem of social evil, turns upon the fact of God's being there. If God is not there (not just the word "God," but God himself being there, the God of the Judaeo-Christian Scriptures), there is no answer at all to the problem of evil and morals. Again, it is not only necessary that he be there, but that he is not silent. There is a philosophic necessity in both metaphysics and morals that he is there and that he is not silent. He has spoken, in verbalized, propositional form, and he has told us what his character is.

Evangelicals often make a mistake today. Without knowing it, they slip over into a weak position. They often thank God in their prayers for the revelation we have of God in Christ. This is good as far as it goes, and it is wonderful that we do have a factual revelation of God in Christ. But I hear very little thanks from the lips of evangelicals today for the propositional revelation in verbalized form which we have in the Scriptures. He must indeed not only be there, but he must have spoken. And he must have spoken in a way which is more than simply a quarry for emotional, upper-story experiences. We need propositional facts. We need to know who he is, and what his character is, because his character is the law of the universe. He has told us what his character is, and this becomes our moral law, our moral standard. It is not arbitrary, for it is fixed in God himself, in what has always been. It is the very opposite of what is relativistic. It is either this or morals are not morals, but simply sociological averages or arbitrary standards imposed by society or the state. It is one or the other.

It is important to remember that it is not improper for men to ask these questions concerning metaphysics and morals, and Christians should point out that there is no answer to these questions except that God is there and he is not silent. Students and other young people should not be told to keep quiet when they ask these questions. They are right to ask them, but we should make it plain to them that these are the only answers. It is this or nothing.

But if this is true, then man is not just metaphysically small, but really morally guilty. He has true moral guilt, and he needs a solution for it. As I have said, it is here that the substitutionary propitiatory death of Christ is needed and fits in. And his death must be substitutionary and propitiatory, or the whole thing has no meaning. There is nothing wrong with man's being metaphysically small, in being finite. This is the way God made him in the first place. But we need a solution for our true moral guilt before the absolutely good God who is there. That is our need.[1]

Finally, as in the area of metaphysics, we must stress that the answer can never lie in the *word* "God"; that will never do. Modern men are trying to find answers just in the word "God," in god-words. This is true of the new theology, the hippie cult and some of the "Jesus people." But the answer is not in the use of the word, but in its *content*: what God has told us concerning himself, as being the infinite-personal God and the true Trinity.

In the area of morals, we have none of these answers except on the basis of a true, space-time, historic fall. There was a time before the fall, and then man turned from his proper integration point by choice, and in so doing, there was a moral discontinuity; man became abnormal. Remove that and the Christian answer in the area of morals is gone. Often I find evangelicals playing games with the first half of Genesis. But if you remove a true, historic, space-time fall, the answers are finished. It is not only that historic, biblical Christianity as it stands in the stream of history is gone, but every answer we possess in the area of morals in the area of man and his dilemma, is gone.

------

[1]Note that in Christianity there is in this area of morals, as in existence, a sufficient answer concerning an original monism but present dualism. This rests on God being good, and creating everything good, but that the nonprogrammed creature revolted and thus brought into existence the present dualism of good and evil. Yet these are not equal, for the evil is contrary to the character of God, which was the original moral monism. Thus, in morals as in existence, there is an answer both for the present dualism yet needed monism.

The
3 Epistemological
Necessity

The Problem

*E*pistemology means the theory of the method or
grounds of knowledge—the theory of knowledge, or how we know, or how we know we
know. Epistemology is the central problem of
our generation; indeed, the so-called "Generation Gap" is really an epistemological gap, simply because the modern generation looks at
knowledge in a way radically different from
previous ones. I have dealt with the reasons for
this at some length in two earlier books,* so will
in this work only touch upon what I covered in
those books concerning Thomas Aquinas and
the dilemma brought about by the development
of his assumptions and system. But here we
shall start farther back than Aquinas, in the
time of the great Greek philosophers.

The Greek philosophers spent much time
grappling with this problem of knowledge, and
the one who wrestled with it most, and with the

Escape from Reason and *The God Who Is There,* Inter-
Varsity Press.

greatest sensitivity, was Plato. He understood the basic problem, and that is that in the area of knowledge, as in the area of morals, there must be more than particulars if there is to be meaning. In the area of knowledge you have *particulars,* by which we mean the individual "things" which we see in the world. At any given moment, I am faced with thousands, indeed literally millions of particulars, just in what I see with a glance of my eyes. What are the universals which give these particulars meaning? This is the heart of the problem of epistemology and the problem of knowing.

A related problem is in our learning. For example, in considering apples, we could list the different varieties every time we spoke of apples, and name two or three hundred kinds. But in practice we draw these all together under the word "apple," and so have a greater comprehension of what we are looking at and what we are talking about. So we are all moving from particulars to universals.

It is much the same in terms of science. Science is looking at the particulars and trying to make laws which cover sufficient numbers of particulars for us to see the association and understand properly. "Super" laws (for example, electromagnetism and gravity) are laws which go further than that, and reduce all the particulars in the material universe to as few universals as possible. So whether we are talking about apples or about science, in learning we are constantly moving from particulars to universals.

This is not only a linguistic thing, it is the *way we know.* It is not just an abstract theory, or some kind of scholasticism, but the matter of actually knowing, and knowing that we know. The Greek philosophers, and especially Plato, were seeking for universals which would make the particulars meaningful.

Now we can understand this very easily in the area of morals. In the previous chapter, I dealt with the area of morals, that we need universals (absolutes) if we are to determine what is right and what is wrong. Not having universals, the modern concept is finally sociological: one assesses the statistics of public opinion of right and wrong, and a majority determines moral questions. Or, we can think of an elite emerging to tell us what is right and what is wrong. But both these approaches are merely matters of *averages.* The Greeks understood that if we were really to know what was right and what was wrong, we had to have a universal which would cover all the particulars.

Now while we can see this more easily in the area of morals, in reality it is even more important in the area of knowledge. How can we find universals which are large enough to cover the particulars so that we can know we know? Plato, for example, put forward the concept of ideals which would provide the needed universal. For example, let us think of chairs: let us say that there is somewhere an ideal chair, and that this ideal chair would cover all the particulars of all the chairs that ever were. Thus a chair had meaning in reference to the ideal chair and not to the particular one. So when we use the word "chair" there is a meaning that is beyond our mere gathering up of the particulars about chairs. This is Plato's solution: an "ideal" somewhere that would cover all the possible particulars that anybody could ever possibly find about chairs. There would be no chairs outside this universal or beyond the concept which was covered by the "ideal" chair. Anything outside of it was not a chair.

From the parallel in the area of morals, we can see the problem of knowledge, of knowing, of being sure. The Greeks thought of two ways to try to come to this. One was the sense of the *polis.* The word *polis* simply means "city," but in Greek thinking the *polis* had meaning beyond merely the geographic city. It had to do with the structure of society. Some Greeks had an idea that the *polis*, the society, could supply the universal. But the Greeks were wise enough soon to see that this was unsatisfactory, because then one is right back to the 51 percent vote or the concept of a small elite. So one would end with Plato's philosopher kings, for example. But this, too, was limited. Even if one only chose the philosopher kings in the *polis*, eventually they are not going to be able to give a universal which would cover all the particulars.

So the next step was to move back to the gods, on the grounds that the gods can give something more than the *polis* can give. But the difficulty is that the Greek gods (and this includes Plato's gods) simply were inadequate. They were personal gods—in contrast to the Eastern gods, who include everything and are impersonal—but they were not big enough. Consequently, because their gods were not big enough, the problem remained unsolved for the Greeks.

Just as society did not solve the problem because it was not big enough, so also the gods did not settle it because they were not big enough. The gods fought among themselves and had differences over all kinds of petty things. All the classical gods put together were not really enough, which is why, as we saw in a previous chapter, in the concept of fate, in Greek literature, one never knows for sure whether the Fates are controlled by the gods, or whether the Fates control the gods. Are the Fates simply the vehicle of the action of the gods or are the Fates the universal behind the gods and do they manipulate the gods? There is this constant confusion between the Fates and the gods as the final control. This expresses the Greeks' deep comprehension that their gods simply were not adequate: they were not big enough with regard to the Fates and they were not big enough with regard to *knowledge*. So though Plato and the Greeks understood the necessity of finding a universal, and saw that unless there was a universal, nothing was going to turn out right, they never found a place from which the universal could come either for the *polis* or for the gods.

Thomas Aquinas picked up the dilemma of the Greek philosophers. Before his time, the Byzantine world had no real interest in particulars. They lived in the midst of them but they had an entirely different thought-form. They were not interested in nature, or in the particulars. We can thank Thomas Aquinas for the fact that because of his view, nature was again brought into importance in man's thinking.

Gradually, as Thomas Aquinas' emphasis spread (as I pointed out in *Escape from Reason*), it began to be understood and disseminated in the area of the arts. Cimabue (1240-1302), for example, began to paint in a different way. Then Dante (1265-1321) began to write in a different way, in which nature had its emphasis. But there was also arising a tension between nature and grace. In nature you have men, and natural cause and effect affecting the world; in grace you have the heavenly forces, and how these unseen forces can affect the world. In nature you have the body; in grace you have the soul. But eventually we always come down to the problem of particulars and universals. In nature you have the particulars; in grace you have the universal. These men, Cimabue and Dante and others, like Giotto (1267-1337) who followed them, began to emphasize nature. This is to the good, as we have said, but there is the problem. There is that which is good, because nature was being reestablished and reemphasized in men's thinking; there is that which is bad, because they were making the particulars autonomous and thus losing the universal that gave the particulars meaning.

As I have emphasized in my previous books, there is a principle here; that is, if nature or the particulars are autonomous from God, then nature begins to eat up grace. Or we could put it in this way: all we are left with are particulars, and universals are lost, not only in the area of morals, which would be bad enough, but in the area of knowing. Here you can see the drift toward modern man and his cynicism. It was born back there. We are left with masses of particulars but no way to get them together. So we find that by this time nature is eating up grace in the area of morals, and even more basically, in the area of epistemology as well.

This is where Leonardo da Vinci is so important. He was the first modern mathematician, and he really understood this dilemma. It is not that I am reading back into him our dilemma of modern cynicism. He really understood it. He understood, in the passage of all these hundreds of years between himself and modern man, where rationalistic man would end up if man failed to find a solution. This is what real genius is—understanding before your time; and Leonardo da Vinci did understand. He understood that if you began on the basis of rationalism —that is, man beginning only from himself, and not having any outside knowledge—you would have only mathematics and particulars and would end up with only mechanics. In other words, he was so far ahead of his time that he really understood that everything was going to end up only as a machine, and there were not going to be any universals or meaning at all. The universals were going to be crossed out. So Leonardo really became very much like the modern man. He said we should try to paint the universals. This is really very close to the modern concept of the upper-story experience. So he painted and painted and painted, trying to paint the universals. He actually tried to paint the universal just as Plato had had the idea that if we were really to have a knowledge of chairs, there would have to be an ideal chair somewhere that would cover all kinds of chairs. Leonardo, who was a Neo-Platonist, understood this, and he said, "Let man produce the universals."

But what kind of men? The mathematical man? No, not the mathematical man but the painter, the sensitive man. So Leonardo is a very crucial man in the area of humanistic epistemology.

At this point in *Escape from Reason* I developed the difference between what I call "modern science" and the "modern modern science."

In my earlier books I have referred to Whitehead and Oppenheimer, two scientists—neither one a Christian— who insisted that modern science could not have been born except in the Christian milieu. Bear with me as I repeat this, for I want in this book to carry it a step further, into the area of knowing. As Whitehead so beautifully points out, these men all believed that the universe was created by a reasonable God and therefore the universe could be found out by reason. This was their base. Modern science is the original science, in which you had men who believed in the uniformity of natural causes in a limited system, a system which could be reordered by God and by man made in the image of God. This is a cause and effect system in a limited time span. But from the time of Newton (not with Newton himself, but with the Newtonians who followed him), we have the concept of the "machine" until we are left with only the machine, and you move into "modern modern science," in which we have the uniformity of natural causes in a closed system, including sociology and psychology. Man is included in the machine. This is the world in which we live in the area of science today. No longer believing that they can be sure the universe is reasonable because created by a reasonable God, the question is raised which Leonardo da Vinci already understood and which the Greeks understood before that: "How does the scientist know; on what basis can he know that what he knows, he really knows?"

So rationalism put forth at this point the epistemological concept of *positivism*. Positivism is a theory of knowing which assumes that we can know facts and objects with total objectivity. Modern "scientism" is built on it.

It is a truly romantic concept, and while it held sway rationalistic man stood ten feet tall in his pride. It was based on the notion that without any universals to begin with, finite man could reach out and grasp with finite reason sufficient true knowledge to make universals out of the particulars.

Jean-Jacques Rousseau is crucial at this point, because he changed the formulation from "nature and grace" to "nature and freedom," absolute freedom. Rousseau and the men around him saw that in the area of "nature," everything had become the machine. In other words, "downstairs" everything was in the area of positivism, and everything was a machine. "Upstairs" they added the other thing, that is, absolute freedom. In the sense of absolute freedom upstairs, not only is man not to be bound by revelation, but he is not to be bound by society, the *polis*, either. This concept of autonomous freedom is clearly seen in Gaugin, the painter. He was getting rid of all the restraints, not just the restraint of God, but also the restraint of the *polis*, which for Gaugin was epitomized by the highly developed culture of France. He left France and went to Tahiti to be rid of the culture, the *polis*. In doing this, he practiced the concept of the noble savage which, of course, Jean-Jacques Rousseau had previously set forth. You get rid of the restraints, you get rid of the *polis*, you get rid of God or the gods; and then you are free. Unhappily, though not surprisingly, this did not turn out as he expected.

So what we have is not a destructive freedom only in morals (though it shows itself very quickly in morals, especially quickly perhaps in sexual anarchy), but in the area of knowledge as well. In metaphysics, in the area of being, as well as morals, we are supposed to have absolute freedom. But then the dilemma comes: how do you know and how do you know you know?

We may imagine the Greeks and Leonardo da Vinci and all the Neo-Platonists at the time of the High Renaissance coming in and asking Rousseau and his followers, "Don't you see what you have done? Where are the universals? How are you going to know? How are you going to build enough universals out of particulars, even for society to run, let alone build true knowledge, knowledge that you really know, and are sure that you know?"

It is only a step, really, from men like Gaugin to the whole hippie culture, and as a matter of fact, to the whole modern culture. In one sense there is a parenthesis in time from Rousseau until the birth of the hippie culture and the whole modern culture which is founded on the view that there are no universals anywhere—that man is totally, hedonistically free, the individual is totally, hedonistically free, not only morally but also in the area of knowledge. We can easily see the moral confusion that has resulted from this, but the epistemological confusion is worse. If there are no universals, how do we know reality from non-reality? At this point, we are right in the lap of modern man's problem, as I will develop later.

Now let us go back to the period immediately after Rousseau, to Immanuel Kant, and Hegel, who changed the whole concept of epistemology. Before this, in epistemology, man always thought in terms of antithesis; the methodology of epistemology had always been antithesis. That is, you learn by saying "a" is not "non-a." That is the first step of classical logic. In other words, in antithesis, if this is true then its opposite is not true. You can make an antithesis. That is the classical methodology of epistemology, of knowing. But Hegel argued that antithesis has never turned out well on a rationalistic basis, so he proposed to change the methodology of epistemology. Instead of dealing with antithesis, let us deal with synthesis. So he set up his famous triangle—everything is a thesis, it sets up an antithesis, and the answer is always synthesis. The whole world changed in the area of morals and political science, but it changed more profoundly, though less obviously, in the area of knowing and knowing itself. He changed the whole theory of how we know.

In my books I move quickly to Kierkegaard, who took this a step further. He set up, as I have indicated, the absolute dichotomy between reason and non-reason. Kierkegaard, and especially Kierkegaardism that followed him, teaches that that which would give meaning is always separated from reason; reason only leads to knowledge downstairs, which is mathematical knowledge without any meaning, but upstairs you hope to find a non-rational meaning for the particulars. This is Kierkegaard's contribution.

All of this flows from four men—Rousseau, Kant, Hegel, and Kierkegaard—and their thinking in the area of epistemology. From Hegel, this kind of thinking has replaced antithesis with synthesis, so turning the whole theory of knowledge upside down. Today, existentialism has three forms: the French, Jean Paul Sartre; the German, Heidegger; and Karl Jaspers, who is also a German but lives in Switzerland. The distinctions between the forms of existentialism do not change the fact that it is the same system even though it has different expressions with these different men, namely, that rationality only leads to something horrible in every area, including knowledge. Indeed, not *including* knowledge, but *first of all* knowledge—*principally* knowledge. To these men as rationalists the knowledge we can know with our reason is only a mathematical formula in which man is only a machine. Instead of reason they hope to find some sort of mystical experience "upstairs," apart from reason, to provide a universal.

Here we can feel again the whole drift of the hippie movement and the drug culture as well. Man hopes to find something in his head because he cannot know certainly that anything is "out there." This is where we are. I am convinced that the generation gap is basically in the area of epistemology. Before, man had a romantic hope that on the basis of rationalism he was going to be able to find a meaning to life, and put universals over the particulars. But on this side of Rousseau, Kant, Hegel, and Kierkegaard, this hope no longer exists; the hope is given up. Young people today live in a generation that no longer believes in the hope of truth as truth. That is why I use the term "true truth" in my books to emphasize real truth. This is not just a tautology. It is an admission that the word "truth" now means something that before these four men would not have been considered truth at all. So in desperation I have coined the expression "true truth" to make the point, but it is hard to make it sharp enough for people to understand how large the problem is.

After Kierkegaard, rationality is seen as leading to pessimism. We can have mathematical knowledge but man is only a machine, and any kind of optimism one could have concerning meaning would have to be in the area of the non-rational, the "upstairs." So rationality, including modern science, will lead only to pessimism. Man is only the machine; man is only a zero, and nothing has any real meaning. I am nothing—one particular among thousands of particulars. No particulars have meaning, and specifically man has no meaning—specifically the particular of myself. I have no meaning; I die; man is dead. If students wonder why they are treated like IBM cards, it is for no less reason than this.

So man makes his leap "upstairs" into all sorts of mysticisms in the area of knowledge—and they *are* mysticisms, because they are totally separated from all rationality. This is a mysticism like no previous mysticism.

Previous mysticisms always assumed something was there. But modern man's mysticisms are semantic mysticisms that deal only with words; they have nothing to do with anything being there, but are simply concerned with something in one's own head, or in language in one form or another. The modern taking of drugs began as one way to try to find meaning within one's head.

The present situation is one where we have in the area of the rational positivism for "scientific fact," that which leads to mathematical formulae and man as a machine; and in the non-rational area we find all kinds of non-rational mysticisms.

Now we must turn our attention again to the "downstairs" positivism. This was the great hope of rationalistic man, but gradually positivism has died. I remember when I first lectured at Oxford and Cambridge, one had to change gears between the two great universities because in Oxford they were still teaching logical positivism, but in Cambridge it was all linguistic analysis. Today it is linguistic analysis almost everywhere in the world. Gradually, positivism has died. For a careful study as to why this has happened, I would recommend Michael Polanyi's book *Personal Knowledge, an Introduction to Post-critical Philosophy.* Polanyi is a name that hardly ever appears in the popular press and he is unknown by many, but he is one of the dominant thinkers in the intellectual world. His book shows why positivism is not a sufficient epistemology, and why the hope of modern science to have any certain knowledge is doomed to failure. And truly there is probably not a chair of philosophy of importance in the world today that teaches positivism. It is still held by the undergraduate and by the naïve scientist who, with a happy smile on his face, is building on a foundation that no longer exists. Now we must notice where we have come. The first of the modern scientists, Copernicus, Galileo, up to Newton and Faraday, as Whitehead pointed out, had the courage to begin to formulate modern science because they believed the universe had been created by a reasonable God and therefore it was possible to find out that which was true about the universe by reason. But when we come to naturalistic science, that is all destroyed; positivism is put in its place, but now positivism itself is destroyed.

Polanyi argues that positivism is inadequate because it does not consider the *knower* of what is known. It acts as though the knower may be overlooked and yet have full knowledge of certain things, as though the knower knew without actually being there. Or you might say positivism does not take into account the knower's theories or presuppositions. You can assume that he approaches the thing without any presuppositions, without any grid through which he feeds his knowledge.

But there is the dilemma, as Polanyi shows, because this simply is not true. There is no scientist in the positivistic position who does not feed knowledge through a grid—a theory or world view through which he sees and finds. The concept of the totally innocent, objective observer is utterly naïve. And science cannot exist without an observer.

When I was younger, people would always say that science is completely objective. Then, some years ago in Oxford it began to be insisted that this is not true; there is no such thing as science without the observer. The observer sets up the experiment and then the observer observes it—then the observer makes the conclusions. Polanyi says the observer is never neutral; he has a grid, he has presuppositions through which he feeds the thing which he finds.

I would go a step further. I have always insisted that positivism has an even more basic problem. One must always judge a system in its own total structure; you cannot mix systems or you get a philosophical chop suey rather than any real thought. Within positivism as a total structure there is no way of saying with certainty that anything exists. Within the system of positivism itself, by the very nature of the case, you simply begin nakedly with nothing there. You have no reason within the system to know that the data is data, or that what is reaching you is data. Within the system there is no universal to give you the right to be sure that what is reaching you from outside is data. The system of positivism itself gives you no certainty that anything is there, or that there is really in the first move any difference between reality and fantasy.

There is a further problem. Not only does the positivist not know certainly that anything is there, but even if it is there he can have no reason to think he knows anything truly nor anywhere near truly. There is no reason within the system to be sure that there is a correlation between the observer—that is, the subject—and the thing—that is, the object.

To bring it further up to date, Karl Popper, who is another of the well-known thinkers of our own day, has until recently argued that a thing is meaningless unless it is open to verification and falsification. But in a recent book he has taken a step backwards. He now says there is *no possibility of verification*. You cannot verify anything—only falsify. That is, you cannot say what a thing is; you can only say certain things that it is not. When Polanyi finished destroying logical positivism so beautifully, he was left with total cynicism in the area of epistemology concerning knowing; in his new book Karl Popper has really come to the same place. In science the same problem is involved with much of the "model" concept. One often finds that the objective reality is getting dim and all that remains is the model in the scientist's head.

We are left then with this. Positivism died and has

been replaced everywhere by linguistic analysis. Positivism did not leave one with knowledge but only with a set of statistical averages and approximations, with no certainty that anything was there finally and no certainty of continuity in the things that were there.

One can relate this to Alfred Korzybski's and D. David Bourland's "General Semantics," which would not allow the verb "to be" ever to be used. All their books are written without the use of the verb "to be." Why? Because they say there is no certainty of continuity. I would add that it seems to me also to be related to the stream of consciousness psychology that ends up with nothing but a stream of consciousness because it is not sure that an "I" is there.

I should like to turn to the philosopher Ludwig Wittgenstein, who is in many ways the key to this whole matter. There is an early Wittgenstein and there is a later Wittgenstein, but in his *Tractatus*, to which we refer here, we are concerned with the early Wittgenstein. Later he moved into linguistic analysis, but in this early stage, he argued that down here in the world (in the area of reason) you have facts: you have the propositions of natural science. This is all that can be said; it is all that you can put into language. This is the limit of language and the limit of logic. "Downstairs" we can speak, but all that can be spoken is the mathematical propositions of natural science. Language is limited to the "downstairs" of reason, and that ends up with mathematical formulations.

But, as Bertrand Russell emphasizes, Wittgenstein was a mystic. Even in his early days, there were already the elements of mysticism. In the "upper story" he put silence, because you could not talk about anything outside of the known world of natural science. But man desperately needed values, ethics, meanings to it all. Man needs these desperately, but there is only silence there. It was at this point that the title of this present book was born. It is Wittgenstein's word "silence" that has given me this title. Wittgenstein says that there is only silence in the area of the things man desperately needs most—values, ethics, and meanings. Man knows it needs to be there, he argues, but he cannot even talk or think about it. Values, ethics, meanings are all upstairs. No matter how much we need them, there is only silence.

From this he plunged into linguistic analysis, which is now the dominant philosophy all over the world. It was born at this place in the desperation that followed when positivism was seen to be inadequate. The "old" Wittgenstein and the existentialist really are very, very close at this particular point, though if you move from England to the Continent in the study of philosophy you find that people usually assume that they are completely at variance. Yet there is a way of looking at them in which they are very close at the moment when Wittgenstein says there is no real value or meaning in all these things, only silence.

For those who know Bergman's film *Silence* this will ring a very familiar bell. Bergman is a philosopher who came to the place where he decided that there would never be anything spoken from this upper level, that God (even as the existentialist would use that word) was meaningless. At that point he made the film *Silence,* and Bergman himself changed from that point onward. In other words, he agreed with what Wittgenstein, the brilliant philosopher, had said many years before. So really Bergman and Wittgenstein must be seen together, and the film *Silence* was a demonstration of this particular point.

What we are left with, let us notice, is an anti-philosophy, because everything that makes life worthwhile, or gives meaning to life, or binds it together beyond isolated particulars is in an "upstairs" of total silence.

Thus we are left with two anti-philosophies in the world today. One is existentialism, which is an anti-philosophy because it deals with the big questions but with no rationality. But if we follow the later Wittgenstein's development, we move into linguistic analysis, and we find that this also is an anti-philosophy, because where it defines words in the area of reason, language leads to language and that is all. It is not only the certainty of values that is gone but the certainty of knowing.

Speaking of Wittgenstein and his moving into the area of language, as we have seen, it is well to mention at this point the later Heidegger, who also dealt with language, though in a very different way. Heidegger was originally an existentialist who believed that there was only the *angst* toward the universe that gave the hope that something was there. But later he moved on into the view that because there was language in the universe, we may hope that there is something there, a nonrational hope of an ultimate meaning to it all. So Heidegger says, "Just listen to the poet," not the *content* of the poet, but listen just because there is a poet who is speaking. In other words, because there is a being—that, is, the poet—who speaks, we can hope that Being—that is, existence—has meaning. He adds a different note in an attempt to make his position empirical and not just abstract. What he did was to claim that there was, in the far past, in the pre-Socratic age before Aristotle, a great, golden language when there was a direct, "first-order experience" from the universe. This was purely hypothetical. It has no base historically, but he proposed it as an act of desperation in an attempt to lay an historical foundation on or under an otherwise purely hypothetical and nebulous concept.

We must understand that these things are not just theoretical in their effects. The later Heidegger is crucially important in theology, in the new hermeneutics. These things have their effect in the student world as well. They are not abstract. They are changing our world.

Let us at this point note an important factor. Whether

we are dealing with Heidegger saying, "Listen to the poet," and offering an upper story semantic mysticism which seems to give hope, or with Wittgenstein who moves in the opposite direction and is more honest in saying that there is only silence upstairs and therefore all we can do is define words which will never deal finally with meanings or values; whether we look at Heidegger or Wittgenstein, who move in opposite directions at the point of language, the interesting thing is that modern man has come to conclude that the secret of the whole thing lies somehow in language. This is the age of semantics at this very basic point.

Notice what this means to us. The whole question with Heidegger and Wittgenstein—and with Bergman—is whether there is anyone adequately there in the universe to *speak*. We are surrounded by a sea of anti-philosophy. Positivism, which was an optimistic rationalism and the base of naturalistic science, has died. It has been proved to be an insufficient epistemology. But the remaining alternatives—existentialism on the one hand, and linguistic analysis on the other—are anti-philosophies which cause man to be hopeless concerning ethics, values, meaning, and the certainty of knowledge. So in epistemology we are surrounded by a sea of anti-philosophy. Polanyi, for example, who was so magnificent in destroying logical positivism, ends up with pure cynicism in the area of epistemology and knowing. So, as we have seen, does Karl Popper. Modern man is stuck right here. Positivism is dead and what is left is cynicism as to knowing. That is where modern man is, whether the individual man knows it or not.

Those who have been raised in the last couple of decades stand right here in the area of epistemology. The really great problem is not, for example, just drugs or amorality. The problem is knowing. This is a generation of anti-philosophy people caught in an uncertainty of knowing. In the downstairs area which modern man ascribes to rationality, and concerning which he talks with meaningful language, he can see himself only as a machine, a totally determined machine, and so has no way to be sure of knowing even the natural world. But in the area of the upstairs, which he ascribes to non-rationality, modern man is completely without categories, for categories are related to reason and antithesis. In the upstairs he has no reason to say that this is right as opposed to that being wrong (or non-right, perhaps, to use the more modern idiom). In the area of morals, in the upstairs he has no way to say one thing is right as opposed to another thing being non-right. But notice it is more profound and more horrible. Equally, living upstairs he has no way to say that this is true as opposed to that which is non-true. Don't you feel the desperation? This means that he has no control (and I use the word "control" with the French meaning, the possibility of checking something), he has no way of having such control in the upstairs.

Now we see this vividly in the cinema. I have dealt with this already at some length in *Escape from Reason* and elsewhere, but it is a necessary part of the picture here, too, and so I am going to repeat myself. Antonioni's film *Blowup* is an example of this. The main character is the photographer. He is a perfect choice because what he is dealing with is not a set of human values but an impersonal photographic lens. The camera could be just as easily hooked up to an impersonal computer as to this photographer. The photographer runs around taking his snapshots, a finite human being dealing only with particulars and totally unable to put any meaning into them, and the cold camera lens offers no judgment, no control in any of what it sees. We recall the posters advertising Antonioni's film: "Murder without guilt, love without meaning." In other words, there are no categories in the area of morals—murder is without guilt; but equally there are no categories in the human realm—love is without meaning. So Antonioni pictures the death of categories.

In the area of morality, there is no universal above; we are left only with particulars. The camera can click, click, click, and we are left with a series of particulars and no universals. That is all that rationalistic man can do for himself, Antonioni says, and he is absolutely right. All the way back to the Greeks, we have for two thousand years the cleverest men who have ever lived trying to find a way to put meaning and certainty of knowledge into the area of rationalistic man, but man, beginning with himself with no other knowledge outside of himself, is a total failure, and Antonioni points it out beautifully in his film.

But the modern cinema and other art forms go beyond the loss of human and moral categories. They point out quite properly that if you have no place for categories, you not only lose categories where moral and human values are concerned, but you also lose any categories which would distinguish between reality and fantasy. This is seen in many modern films and novels, for example *Belle de Jour*, *Juliet of the Spirits*, *In the Balance*, *Rendezvous*, and— closest to our own moment as I write this, and very well done—the film of Bergman, *The Hour of the Wolf*.

The drug culture enters into this too. At the very heart of the thing is the loss of distinction between reality and fantasy by the taking of drugs. But even if modern man does not take drugs, he has no categories once he has moved out of the lower area of reason. Downstairs he is already dead; he is only a machine, and none of these things have any meaning. But as soon as he moves upstairs into the area of the upper-story mysticism, all that is left is a place with no categories with which to distinguish the inner world from the outer world with any certainty or to distinguish what is in his head from that which is in the external world.

What we are left with today is the fact that modern man has no categories to enable him to be at all sure of the difference between what is real and what is only in his head. Many who come to us at L'Abri have suffered this loss of distinction between reality and fantasy.

There are four groups of categories involved here. We have considered three of these: first, the moral category; second, the human; third, the categories of reality and fantasy. The fourth, which we examine now, concerns our knowing other people.

The third group of categories is concerned with moving from inside the head to outside the head with certainty, and being sure that there is any difference between reality and fantasy. The fourth group is the reverse—how can two people meeting ever know each other—moving from outside their heads into each other's heads? How do we have any categories to enable us to move into the other person's thought world? This is the modern man's alienation; this is the blackness which so many modern people face, the feeling of being totally alienated. A couple can sleep together for ten or fifteen years, but how are they going to get inside each other's heads to know anything about the other person as a person, in contrast merely to a language machine? It is easy to know the façade of a language machine, but how can you get in behind the language and know the person in this kind of setting? This is a very special modern form of lostness.

I had this brought strongly to my attention a number of years ago when a very modern couple came to L'Abri. We put them in one of the chalets. They kept everyone awake night after night because they would talk all the way through the night, until morning—talk, talk, talk. They were driving everyone crazy. Naturally, I became intrigued. I wondered what they were talking about. These people had been together for a long time; what did they talk about all the time? When I got to know them I found out, and it turned on a new dimension for me as it dawned on me what the dilemma really is. I found out that they talked because they were trying desperately to know each other. They were really in love, and they were talking and talking in order to try to find one sentence or one phrase which they could know *exhaustively* together so that they could begin to know each other and to move inside of each other's heads. They had no universals in their world and thus they had to make a universal by a totally exhaustive point of contact. Being finite, they could not reach this.

So how do you begin? You are left with only particulars. Moving outward, you have no certainty that there is anything there, outside. Moving inside, inward, you are trying to move into somebody else's head. How do you know you are touching him? In this setting, human beings are the only ones who are there. There is no one else there to speak—only silence. So if you do not have the exhaustive phrase, how do you begin? You just cannot begin by knowing something partially, it must be exhaustive because there is no one else anywhere to provide any universals. The universal, the certainty, must be in your own conversation, in one exhaustive sentence or one exhaustive phrase to begin with. The problem is in the area of epistemology and it centers on language.

Modern man is left either downstairs as a machine with words that do not lead either to values or facts but only to words, or he is left upstairs in a world without categories in regard to human values, moral values, or the difference between reality and fantasy. Weep for our generation! Man, made in the image of God and intended to be in vertical communication with the One who is there and who is not silent, and meant to have horizontal communication with his own kind, has, because of his proud rationalism, making himself autonomous, come to this place.

I would end this chapter with a quotation from *Satyricon* of Fellini. Toward the end of the film, a man looks down at his friend who is dying a ridiculous death, an absolutely absurd death. With all his hopes, he has come to a completely absurd end. Modern man, made in the image of God and meant to be in communication with God and then with his kind, has come to this place of horrible silence. In the film Fellini has the voice say, "O God, how far he lies from his destination now." There was never a truer word.

The
4 Epistemological Necessity

The Answer

*T*here is a Christian answer to the epistemological problem. Let us begin by remembering that the High Renaissance had a problem of nature and grace: their rationalism and humanism had no way to bind nature and grace together. They never achieved an answer to the problem, and the dilemma of the twentieth century really springs from this. Rationalistic and humanistic men, brilliant as they were, could never find the way to bind nature and grace together. However, at about the same time, as I have emphasized in my earlier books, the Reformation was taking place, and the Reformation had no problem of nature and grace. This is really a tremendous distinction. Nature and grace arose as a problem out of the rationalistic, humanistic Renaissance and it has never been solved. It is not that Christianity had a tremendous problem at the Reformation, and that the reformers wrestled with all this and then came up with an answer. No, there simply *was no problem of nature and grace* to the Reformation, because the Reformation had verbal, propositional revelation, and there was no dichotomy between nature and grace. The historic Christian position had no nature and grace problem because of propositional revelation, and revelation deals with language.

In our own generation, we have reached the core of the problem of language. We have already discussed the later Heidegger's use of language, and also Wittgenstein's use of language and linguistic analysis. But the difference is that Heidegger and Wittgenstein realized that there must be something spoken if we are going to know anything, but they had no one there to speak. It is as simple and as profound as that. Is there anyone there to speak? Or do we, being finite, just gather enough facts, enough particulars, to try to make our own universals?

In the Reformation and the Judaeo-Christian position in general, we find that there is someone there to speak, and that he has told us about two areas. He has spoken first about himself, not exhaustively but truly; and second, he has spoken about history and about the cosmos, not exhaustively but truly. This being the case, and as he has told us about both things on the basis of propositional, verbalized revelation, the Reformation had no nature and grace problem. They had a unity, for the simple reason that revelation spoke to both areas, thus the problem simply did not exist. Rationalism could not find an answer, but God, speaking, gives the unity needed for the nature and grace dilemma.

This brings us to a very basic question. Is the biblical position intellectually possible? Is it possible to have intellectual integrity while holding to the position of verbalized, propositional revelation? I would say the answer is this: It is not possible if you hold the presupposition of the uniformity of natural causes in a closed system. If you do, any idea of revelation becomes nonsense. It is not only that there are problems, in such a case, but that it becomes absolute nonsense if you really believe in the uniformity of natural causes in a closed system, namely, that *everything* is a machine. Whether you begin with a naturalistic view in philosophy or a naturalistic view in theology makes no difference. For the liberal theologian, it is quite impossible to think of real propositional revelation. Discussion only about detail is not going to solve the problem. The big thing has to be faced, the question of the presuppositions. If I am completely committed, without question, to the uniformity of natural causes in a closed system, then whether I express myself in philosophical or religious terms, propositional, verbalized revelation—knowledge that man has from God—is a totally unthinkable concept. This is because by definition everything is a machine, so naturally there is no knowledge from outside—from God. If this is your world view, and you refuse to consider the possibility of any other, even though your naturalistic world view leads to the dehumanization of man and is against the facts that we know about man and things, you are at a dead end. You must remember you can only hold the uniformity of natural causes in the closed system, which is the monolithic consensus today, by denying what man knows about man. But if you insist upon holding this view, even though it dehumanizes man, and even though it is opposed to the evidence of what man knows about man, then you must understand there is no place for revelation. Not only that, but if you are going to hold to the uniformity of natural causes in the closed system, against all the evidence (and I do insist it is against the evidence), then you will never, never be able to consider the other presupposition which began modern science in the first place: the uniformity of natural causes in a *limited* system, open to reordering by God and by man.

There is an interesting factor here, and that is that in

modern, secular anthropology (and I stress secular), the distinction of man against non-man is made in the area of language. It was not always so. The distinction used to be made in the area of man as the tool maker, so that wherever you found the tool maker it was man as against non-man. This is no longer true. The distinction is now language. The secular anthropologists agree that if we are to determine what is man in contrast to what is non-man it is not in the area of tool making, but in the area of the verbalizer. If it is a verbalizer, it is man. If it is a non-verbalizer, it is not man.

We have now concluded that what marks man as man is verbalization. We communicate propositional communication to each other in spoken or written form in language. Indeed, it is deeper than this because the way we think inside of our own heads is in language. We can have other things in our heads besides language, but it always must be linked to language. A book, for example, can be written with much figure of speech, but the figure of speech must have a continuity with the normal use of syntax and a defined use of terms, or nobody knows what the book is about. So whether we are talking about outward communication or inward thought, man is a verbalizer.

Now let us look at this argument from a non-Christian view, from the modern man's view of the uniformity of natural causes in a closed system. Here all concept of propositional revelation, and especially verbalized propositional revelation, is totally nonsense. The question I have often tried to raise in connection with this presupposition of the uniformity of natural causes in a closed system is whether it is viable in the light of what we know. I would insist it is not. It fails to explain man. It fails to explain the universe and its form. It fails to stand up in the area of epistemology.

It is obvious that propositional, verbalized revelation is not possible on the basis of the uniformity of natural causes. But the argument stands or falls upon the question: Is the presupposition of the uniformity of natural causes really acceptable? In my earlier books and in the previous chapters of this book we have considered whether this presupposition is in fact acceptable, or even reasonable, not upon the basis of Christian faith, but upon the basis of what we know concerning man and the universe as it is.

Christianity offers an entirely different set of presuppositions. The other presuppositions simply do not meet the need. Let us say, by the way, that one must be careful of words. In Britain, for instance, presupposition is sometimes a difficult word. A presupposition is something you do not know you have. But that is not the way I use the word. I use presupposition as a base and we can choose it. Many people do get their presuppositions from their family or from society without knowing it, but it does not need to be this way. What I urge people to do is to consider the two great presuppositions—the uniformity of natural causes in a closed system and the uniformity of natural causes in an open system, in a limited time span—and to consider which of these fits the facts of what is.

Christianity has a different set of presuppositions. It begins with a God who is there, who is the infinite-personal God, who has made man in his image. He has made man to be the verbalizer in the area of propositions in his horizontal communication to other men. Even secular anthropologists say that somehow or other, they do not know why, man is the verbalizer. You have something different in man. The Bible says, and the Christian position says, "I can tell you why: God is a personal-infinite God." There has always been communication, before the creation of all else, in the Trinity. And God has made man in his own image, and part of making man in his own image is that man is the verbalizer. That stands in the unity of the Christian structure.

Now let us ask ourselves this question: In the Christian structure, would it be unlikely that this personal God who is there and made man in his own image as a verbalizer, in such a way that he can communicate horizontally to other men on the basis of propositions and language—is it unthinkable or even surprising that this personal God could or would communicate to man on the basis of propositions? The answer is, no. I have never met an atheist who thought that this would be regarded as surprising within the Christian structure. Indeed, it is what one would expect. If God has made us to be communicators on the basis of verbalization, and given the possibility of propositional, factual communication with each other, why should we think he would not communicate to us on the basis of verbalization and propositions? In the light of the total Christian structure, it is totally reasonable. Propositional revelation is not even surprising, let alone unthinkable, within the Christian framework.

The personal God has made us to speak to each other in language. So if a personal God has made us to be language communicators—and that is obviously what man is —why then should it be surprising to think of him speaking to Paul in Hebrew on the Damascus Road? Why should it be a surprise? Do we think God does not know Hebrew? Equally, if the personal God is a good God, why should it be surprising, in communicating to man in a verbalized, propositional, factual way, that he should tell us the true truth in all areas concerning which he communicates?* It is only surprising if you have been infiltrated by the presuppositions of uniformity of natural causes in a closed system. Then, of course, it is impossible. But as I have said, it is a question of which of these two sets of presuppositions really and empirically meets the facts as we look about us in the world.

---

*For a more extended consideration of verbalized, propositional revelation, see Appendix 1: "Is Propositional Revelation Nonsense?"

What we now find is that the answer rests upon language in revelation. Christianity has no nature and grace problem, and the reason for this rests upon language in revelation. The amazing thing is that Heidegger and Wittgenstein, two of the great names in the area of modern epistemology, both understand that the answer would be in the area of language, but they have no one there to speak.

Christianity has no problem of nature and grace. But let me add, very gently, Christianity has no problem of epistemology either. Remember Chapter 3 and the absolute agony of modern man in the area of knowing, in epistemology—the utter, utter blackness of what is involved. To the Christian, there is no problem in the area of epistemology, just as there is no problem in the area of nature and grace. It is not that we happen to have an answer, but rather that there is no problem in the Christian structure.

Let us be clear as to why there is no problem of epistemology in the Christian structure. From the Christian viewpoint, we must come back and grasp really deeply what Oppenheimer and Whitehead have said about the birth of modern science.

May I remind you of a point I made in an earlier chapter. Whitehead and Oppenheimer said modern science could not have been born except in the milieu of Christianity. Why? In the area of biblical Christianity, Galileo, Copernicus, Kepler, Francis Bacon—all these men, up to Newton and Faraday—understood that there was a universe there because God had made it. And they believed, as Whitehead has so beautifully said, that because God was a reasonable God one could discover the truth of the universe by reason. So modern science was born. The Greeks had almost all the facts that the early scientists had, but it never turned into a science like modern science. This came, as Whitehead said, out of the fact that these men really were sure that the truth of the universe could be pursued in reason because it had been made by a reasonable God.

As I have stressed over and over again, I do not believe for a moment that if the men back at that point of history had had the philosophy, the epistemology of modern man, there would ever have been modern science. I really do not. I think science is going to die, too. I think its death is coming. I think it is going to be reduced to two things: mere technology, and another form of sociological manipulation.* I do not believe for a moment that science is going to be able to continue with its objectivity once the base that brought forth science has been totally destroyed, and now that the hope of positivism has also been destroyed. I do not think it is going to hold on. But one thing I am sure of, and that is that science never would have begun if men had had the uncertainty that modern man has in the area of epistemology. There would have been no way to take with certainty the first steps which these men were able to take.

Now notice that when we carry this over into epistemology, the position is exactly the same. It was because the infinite-personal God who exists—not just an abstraction—made things together, that the early scientists had courage to expect to find out the explanation of the universe. The God who is there made the universe, with things together, *in relationships*. Indeed, the whole area of science turns upon the fact that he has made a world in which things are made to stand together, that there are relationships between things. So God made the external universe, which makes true science possible, but he has also made man and made him to live in that universe. He has not made man to live somewhere else. So we have three things coming together: God, the infinite-personal God, who made the universe; and man, whom he made to

---

*I have developed this thought in *The Church at the End of the Twentieth Century*, Inter-Varsity Press.

live in that universe; and the Bible, which he has given us to tell us about that universe. Are we surprised that there is a unity between them? Why should we be surprised?

So he made the universe, he made man to live in that universe, and he gives us the Bible, the verbalized, propositional, factual revelation, to tell us what we need to know. In the Bible he not only tells us about morals, which makes possible real morals instead of merely sociological averages, but he gives us comprehension to correlate our knowledge. The reason the Christian has no problem of epistemology is exactly the same as the reason why there is for the Christian no problem of nature and grace. The same reasonable God made both things, namely, the known and the knower, the subject and the object, and he put them together. So it is not surprising if there is a correlation between these things. Is that not what you would expect?

If modern science could be born on the basis of there being a reasonable God, which makes it possible to find out the order by reason, should we be taken by surprise that the knower who is to know and the object which is to be known should have a correlation? It is exactly what we should expect. Because we have a reasonable God who made them in the first place there is a reasonable correlation between the subject and the object.

In the previous chapter we saw that the really basic horror of great darkness for modern man is that he cannot have any certainty of the relationship of the subject and the object. But the Christian position starts from another set of presuppositions altogether, that there is a reason for a correlation between the subject and the object. Now, interestingly, this is not against human experience. This is the experience of all men. If it were some mystical, religious thing that somebody offers as a leap completely out of reality and with no way to test it objectively, it would indeed be just one more piece of pie in the sky. But it does not matter how theoretically unrelated a man in his philosophy is, in reality he lives as though there is correlation between the subject and the object. Remember Godard's film, where you may perhaps go out through the windows instead of the doors, but you do not go out through the solid walls.

The fact is that if we are going to live in this world at all, we must live in it acting on a correlation of ourselves and the thing that is there, even if one has a philosophy that there is no correlation. There is no other way to live in this world. That is true for everybody, even the most "unrelated man" you have ever seen, the man who says there is no correlation. It does not matter a bit. He lives in this world on the basis of his experience that there is a correlation between the subject and the object. He not only lives that way, he *has* to live that way. There is no other way to live in this world. That is the way the world is made. So just exactly as all men love even if they say love does not exist, and all men have moral motions, even though they say moral motions do not exist, so all men act as though there is a correlation between the external and the internal world, even if they have no basis for that correlation.

What I am saying is that the Christian view is exactly in line with the experience of every man, but no other system except the Judaeo-Christian one—that which is given in the Old and New Testaments together—tells us why there is a subject-object correlation that one does and must act on. Everybody does act on it, everybody must act on it, but no other system tells you why there is a correlation between the subject and the object. In other words, all men constantly and consistently act as though Christianity is true.

Let me draw the parallel again. Modern men say there is no love, there is only sex, but they fall in love. Men say there are no moral motions, everything is behavioristic, but they all have moral motions. Even in the more profound area of epistemology, no matter what a man says he believes, actually—every moment of his life—he is acting as though Christianity were true and it is only the Christian system that tells him why he can, must, and does act the way he does. There is no other way.

Though man is different from other things, in that man is made in the image of God and other things are not (he has personality, "mannishness," in my own word) yet nevertheless he is as much a creature as the other things. They and he are equally created. At this level they are equal, on the level of creaturehood. It follows, therefore, that though we are separated from other created things by personality, nevertheless we are fellow creatures in a common world because God made it that way.

If you read my application of this argument to the subject of ecology, *Pollution and the Death of Man, The Christian View of Ecology,** you will remember how I developed this point. In the area of ecology, I argue that because we are fellow creatures, we are to treat the tree, the animal, and the air properly. That, I believe, is the Christian basis of ecology. Now, in epistemology, do you not feel that it is just a step further? In epistemology, this fellow creature is the object and I am the subject. We are both made by the same reasonable God and hence I can know my fellow creature truly. In ecology, I am to treat it well, according to the way God made it. I am not to exploit it. But it is deeper than this. I am not only to treat it well, but I can *know* it truly as a fellow creature.

In epistemology we know the thing is there because God made it to be there. It is not an extension of his essence, it is not a dream of God as much Eastern thinking says things are. It is really there. It has a true objective re-

*Tyndale House Publishers.

ality, and we are not surprised to find that there is a correlation between the observer and the observed because God made them to go together. They are made by the same God in the same frame of reference. God made them together, the subject and the object, the knower and the known, and he made them in the same frame of reference. The Christian simply does not have a problem with epistemology. And every man lives as though it is true, regardless of what he says in his epistemological theories. The Christian is not surprised that the tree is there, and he is not surprised that he cannot walk through it, because he knows the tree is really there.

Now everybody has to face this truth, whether it is a very intellectual man who might hate the Christian view, or whether it is the very simple one who lives as though the Christian view is true simply because he acts that way without asking any questions. To both of these the Christian says, what do you expect? Naturally this is the way it is, because the reasonable God made both the subject and the object. He makes the subject and he makes the object, and he gives us the Bible to give us the needed knowledge.

When Michael Polanyi destroyed positivism so magnificently, as we pointed out in an earlier chapter, he was left with only cynicism. But the Christian is not left with cynicism in regard to the subject-object relationship because the same God made them both. Therefore, the correlation between them is not a surprise to the Christian.

However, there is a question raised that we must deal with at this point. That is, how we should consider the problem of the accuracy of knowledge. All these things relate to language, which introduces the modern subject of semantics and linguistic analysis, not as a philosophy but as a tool. It can be at certain points a helpful tool if one consciously rejects it as a rationalistic philosophy. Indeed, the subject-object relationship and the problem of language are related in a very real way.

Now, we must realize that there are three possible views of language. The first is that because we bring our own backgrounds to every word we ever use, every sentence we ever say, it means that we cannot communicate at all. Our own backgrounds so mark our words and our phrases that they just do not touch.

The opposite is that as soon as we use any term in a symbol system of language, everybody has an exhaustive, absolute, and common meaning of that term because we are all using the same words.

So here we have these two extreme views, neither adequate.

Your terms are so marked by your past experience that they do not touch at all, or else every term automatically has an exhaustive meaning, common to the speaker and hearer. But obviously neither of these two views, these extreme views, is an adequate explanation of what really happens in language. In reality, how do we find that language operates in the world? Surely we find it is like this: Though we do bring our own backgrounds to language, which gives the word a special cast out of our own backgrounds, yet there is also, with reasonable care, enough overlapping on the basis of the external world and the human experience to ensure that we can communicate even though we fall short of an exhaustive meaning of the same word. In other words, our words overlap, even while they do not fit completely. And that is the way we all operate in the area of language.

The illustration I like to use here concerns the word "tea." "Tea" is a symbol in our English linguistic symbol system representing a real, identifiable object. But my wife was born in China and her first experience of the thing which t-e-a represents (in our linguistic symbol system) was in Chinese homes. There the Chinese taught her something that she remembers to this day, that the way to drink tea is to drink it from a bowl with a mouthful of rice which you pack into one cheek. In fact, you learn to drink the tea around the rice without touching or disturbing it. To her, that is all bound up in her word "tea."

But for me "tea" begins with me and my mother in Germantown, Philadelphia, making tea in a way I would not make it today, with an aluminum tea caddy that you put into the water. These things mark the word "tea" to both of us, but do you think for a moment that because we have these different connotations, these different shadows on the word "tea," that I cannot say to my wife, "Dear, will you please bring me a pot of tea?" and I do not get a pot of tea? Do you understand what I have said? If you are wrestling with semantics and linguistic analysis, you had better understand this. Keep away from the two extremes; recognize that there are overlaps in our external world and in our common, human experience.

This is true with language, and we must also realize it is true with knowing. We do not have to choose between these two extremes, either in language or epistemology. We can know truly without knowing exhaustively. As long as the thing is there, and I am there in correlation with that other thing, I do not have to know it exhaustively. After all, this does not surprise us because we come down to the fact that nobody knows anything exhaustively except God; *nobody.*

So we notice that, just as in the area of language, there is enough overlap to enable us to communicate with each other. We do not need to have exhaustive knowledge of a thing in order to know truly as long as it is there, I am there, and we have sufficient correlation together. In the Christian background we are all creatures of God and we live in his world. When we use words, we do not exhaust them, even words like "house" or "dog." These are not exhausted between one person and another, and yet though they have personal overtones we can communicate in an accurate if not an exhaustive way.

We should not be surprised if the same thing is true in our knowing, not in hearing a spoken word but in the subject-object relationship. We are not surprised if we do not know the object exhaustively, but neither are we surprised if we find that we can know it truly. If the same reasonable God made both the subject and the object, we are not surprised that there is a correlation between them.

So we have seen why Christianity has no problem of epistemology at all. In past ages, when people were working on a Christian base, epistemology was never discussed with the awful tension which surrounds it today. Men studied many of these questions and the details of them, but there was none of this dilemma that is so common today. The reason for the modern dilemma is that men have moved from uniformity of natural causes in an open system—open to reordering by God and man—into the uniformity of natural causes in a closed system. With that, epistemology dies. But on a Christian basis, there is no problem.

What follows from this? Three things: First of all, here am I, looking outward. Although that is a very simple way to put it, it nevertheless represents the basic problem of epistemology. How can I have any certain knowledge, or knowledge in general, or knowledge of knowledge in general; and secondly, how can I distinguish between knowledge of what is there objectively in contrast to hallucination and illusion?

Clearly, there are borderline cases. Brain injury, schizophrenia, and other forms of mental illness may blur the distinction between objective reality and fantasy. Of course, the taking of drugs can produce a similar condition. Whether it is a psychological illness or an artificially imposed mental schizophrenia caused by drugs, the Christian sees it as a symptom of the Fall. Things are not completely the way God made them in the first place. There are alienations between man and God, between man and himself, and between man and nature. All this is a result of the Fall, so it is not surprising that there are borderline cases in the realm of true knowledge and fantasy.

Nevertheless, the Christian is in an entirely different situation from modern man, for instance, from the thinking behind Antonioni's *Blowup* as we considered it earlier. The Christian has a certainty right from the start that there is an external world that is there, created by God as an objective reality. He is not like the man who has nowhere to begin, who is not sure that there is anything there. The dilemma of positivism, as I have shown, is that, within its own system, it must start without any knowledge that there is anything there. The Christian is not in this position. He knows it is going to be there because God has made it there. The reason why the East never produced a science on its own is that Eastern thinking has never had a certainty of the objective existence of reality. Without an external world there is no subject for scientific study, no basis for experiment or deduction. But the Christian, being sure of the reality of the external world, has a basis for true knowledge. Even though we must acknowledge that we live in a fallen world, and there are abnormalities and borderline cases, yet the Christian is not sucked into the dilemma with which Antonioni wrestles in *Blowup*.

Not only that, but the Christian can live in the world that God has made. This must be the test, after all. That is the difference between science and science fiction. Science must fit into the world that is there; it cannot be isolated from it.

It is not surprising that if a reasonable God created the universe and put me in it, he should also give a correlation of *the categories of my mind* to fit that which is there, simply because I have to live in it. This is a logical extension of my previous points. If this world is made the way the Judaeo-Christian system says it is made, we should not be surprised that man should have categories of the mind to fit the universe in which he lives.

There is a great deal of work being done today on the subject of uniform categories in the human mind, by men like Claude Levi-Strauss, for example, or Noam Chomsky in his idea of basic grammar. These men are finding that somehow or other there are uniform categories of the human mind. But the Christian says, What do you expect? The personal-infinite God who has made the world and has put me into it, is naturally going to make the categories of mind to fit the place where he put me.

Let us bring this over into the physical world. I have a lung system, and the lung system fits the earth atmosphere in which I live. It would not fit Venus or Mars and it does not fit the moon, but it fits my own environment. Why does it fit the world in which I live? It is not surprising that my lung system is in correlation to the world's atmosphere, for the same reasonable God made both my lung system and the atmosphere and he put me in this world. So we should expect a correlation between my lung system and the atmosphere in which I live. Going back to the area of epistemology, there is no surprise that God has given me a correlation between the categories of my mind and the world in which I live. Thus in the matter of knowledge, if a reasonable God made the world and has also made me, we are not surprised if he made the categories of the human mind to fit into the categories of the external world. Both are his creation. There are categories in the external world and there are categories of my mind. Should I be surprised if they fit?

This, of course, is very different from positivism, which has nothing in its system to explain why anything is there. As I said previously, positivism of all forms died because the word "data" is a faith word to positivism. There is nothing inherent in the system to explain why data would be there. It is exactly opposite to the Christian position.

Let us notice another element in the biblical position in this matter of categories. The Bible teaches in two different ways: first, it teaches certain things in didactic statements, in verbalizations, in propositions. For example, it teaches me in didactic terms the principles we have been dealing with in this book. Second, the Bible teaches by showing how God works in the world that he himself made. We should read the Bible for various reasons. It should be read for facts, and it should also be read devotionally. But reading the Bible every day of one's life does something else—it gives one a different mentality. In the modern world we are surrounded by the mentality of the uniformity of natural causes in a closed system, but as we read the Bible it gives us a different mentality. Do not minimize the fact that in reading the Bible we are living in a mentality which is the right one, opposed to the great wall of this other mentality which is forced upon us on every side—in education, in literature, in the arts, and in the mass media.

When I read the Bible, I find that when the infinite-personal God himself works in history and in the cosmos, he works in a way which confirms what he has said about the external world. That is what I call the covenant of creation. What he does never violates what he tells us. When God works in the flow of history, he works consistently with the way he says the external world is. The universal working into the particulars defines and confirms what he says the particulars are.

So in the Bible we have two things—we have the didactic teaching of the Scripture, and we also have that which makes us say, "Yes, God works that way." This is a very profound concept indeed. There are miracles in the Bible, but the great stretch of the Bible is not made up of miracles. They are unusual happenings, and that is why we call them miracles. Usually we find God working in the world within the natural laws of the world as he made it. The Red Sea is pushed back; he uses the east wind. Jesus would cook a fish, so there is a fire to cook the fish on. Here and there, there are indeed miracles, but for the most part God acts in the world in a way that confirms both my observations of the world, and also the way God says it is in the didactic portions of the Bible.

These two eyes which the Bible gives us to look through always agree perfectly—the eye of didactic teaching and the eye of God working into history and in the cosmos. This is parallel to that profound statement in the Westminster Confession of Faith, that when God reveals his attributes to man, they are true not only to man but to God. God is not just telling a story; he is telling us what is really true to himself. What he tells us is not exhaustive, because we are finite and we know nothing in an exhaustive way. We cannot even communicate with each other exhaustively, because we are finite. But he tells us truly—even the great truth about himself. He is not playing games with us.

On this same basis we find that science need not be a game. Science today is changing; it is becoming a game. As I have said, I do not believe for a moment that science, which has given up the thing which began it, and now has lost its positivism as well, can continue in a really objective way. Science becomes a game in two different ways. With many a scientist, science becomes a kind of gamemanship. He is playing a complicated game within a very limited area so that he never has to think of the real problems or of meaning. There is many a scientist in his laboratory who has shut himself up to the reading on the dials, and the *specimen* all but disappears. This is no more than another bourgeois gamemanship to fill up the time, like a rich playboy skiing downhill, downhill, for perhaps thirty years, watching only the second hand on his watch. But for the Christian the world has meaning; it has objective reality. Science is no longer a game.

The second and more terrifying way, I think, is the headlong rush towards sociological science.* Because men have lost the objective basis of certainty of knowledge of the thing in which they are working, more and more I fear we are going to find them manipulating science according to their own sociological or political desires rather than standing upon concrete objectivity. I think we are going to find more and more what I would call sociological science, where we find men manipulating the scientific facts. The loss of the certainty of objectivity is a serious thing to the scientist just as it is for the hippie. We can see it in the hippie—he has often lost the distinction between reality and fantasy; the objectivity is gone, with or without drugs. We feel like crying for these people, and we should be crying. But the scientist is often in the same place. If he loses the epistemological base, he, too, is in a serious position. What does science mean any more—once you are no longer sure of the objectivity of the thing, or you are no longer on an epistemological base which gives the certainty of a correlation between the subject and the object?

But the Christian expects to touch the real, to find out about it, and distinguish the real from the non-real, just as the early scientists did. This is where we stand. When the Christian does reach out without cynicism in the area of knowing, the external world really *is* there. Why? Because God made it to be there, and he made a correlation between the subject and the object. That is I, looking outward.

The second result of the Christian view of epis-

*See *The Church at the End of the Twentieth Century*, Inter-Varsity Press.

temology concerns others looking at me: what I am, the inward reality of my thought world, in contrast to what I seem to be from the viewpoint of others. This is a horrible problem for many modern young people. They are always trying to know each other, and all they find is a façade. How do you get behind this? How do you get behind, to the real person who is there?

The Christian does not have to choose between knowing the external or inward worlds totally, or not knowing them at all. I must not expect to know this other man perfectly, because I am finite. But I may expect what I do know to fit together because, after all, the same One has made it all. The strength of the Christian system—the acid test of it—is that everything fits under the apex of the existent, infinite-personal God, and it is the only system in the world where this is true. No other system has an apex under which everything fits. That is why I am a Christian and no longer an agnostic. In all the other systems something "sticks out," something cannot be included; and it has to be mutilated or ignored. But without losing his own integrity, the Christian can see everything fitting into place beneath the Christian apex of the existence of the infinite-personal God who is there.

This is true when I am looking out at the world, but it is also true as I look inward to other people in this desperately important area that occupies so much of the thinking of young people. How can they know other people? How are they going to get beyond this wooden façade? How does one know there is anything back there? What about the contrast between what I may be inside, what I am inside, and what I appear outwardly? How can I know anyone else?

The biblical revelation, according to God's teachings, binds not only the outward man but the inward man as well. The norms of Scripture are not just for the outward man,

but also for the inward man. In the Old Testament, what is
the last commandment? It is internal: "You shall not covet."
This concerns the inward man. Without this, all the rest falls
to the ground. God's Ten Commandments bind not only the
outward man in regard to *morals*, but the inward man too;
and God's giving of *knowledge* where it touches history and
the cosmos binds not only the outward man, but the inward
man, and in these there is a unity.

We find, therefore, that the Bible gives a propositional, factual revelation of God in norms both for the inward and the outward man. The inward man, according to
the Bible, is not autonomous, any more than the outward
man is autonomous. Every time the inward man becomes
autonomous, it is just as much a revolution as when the
outward man becomes autonomous. Every human problem,
as I have stressed in an earlier book,* arises from man's
trying to make something autonomous from God, and as I
have emphasized, as soon as anything is made autonomous
from God, then nature eats up grace.

We have the same thing in the area of knowing other
people. Nothing is to be autonomous from God. The inward areas of knowledge, meaning, and values, and the inward areas of morals, are bound by God as much as the
outward world. As the Christian grows spiritually he
should be a man who consciously, more and more, brings
his thought world as well as his outward world under the
norms of the Bible. But what about the non-Christian? As
a Christian approaches the non-Christian, he still has a
starting place from which to know the person in a way that
the non-Christian does not have, because he knows who
the person is. One of the most brilliant men I have ever
worked with sat in my room in Switzerland crying, simply
because he had been a real humanist and existentialist. He
had gone from his home in a South American country to

*Escape from Reason, Inter-Varsity Press.

Paris, because this was the center of all this great humanistic thought. But he found it was so ugly. The professors cared nothing. It was inhuman in its humanism. He was ready to commit suicide when he came to us. He said, "How do you love me, how do you start?" I said I could start. "I know who you are," I told him, "because you are made in the image of God." We went on from there. Even with a non-Christian, the Christian has some way to begin: to go from the façade of the outward to the reality of the inward, because no matter what a man says he is, we know who he *really* is. He is made in the image of God; that's who he is. And we know that down there somewhere—no matter how wooden he is on the outside, or how much he has died on the outside, no matter if he believes he is only a machine—we know that beyond that façade there is the person who is a verbalizer and who loves and wants to be loved. And no matter how often he says he is amoral, in reality he has moral motions. We know that because he has been made in the image of God. Hence, even with a non-Christian, the Christian has a way to start, from the outside to the inside, in a way that non-Christians simply do not have.

But among Christians there should be a more profound way to know each other. Let us say we want to have communication, we are sick of this horrible mechanical inhumanity that we find around us. We are sick of being simply IBM cards. The Christian boy and girl who want to be open with each other, the Christian husband and wife who want to be open with each other, the pastor and the people who want to be open with each other —how can they really do it, moving from the outside inward? The problem of knowing each other is the discrepancy between what a man seems to be and what he is inside. That is always the problem with getting inside and getting to know each other. So, how do you get through?

Can you see that to the extent to which people accept biblical teaching for the inward man as well as the outward man, there is an increasing integration of the inward and the outward man—because they see both the inward and the outward man under the unity of the same norms, in regard to both values and knowing? It is possible to move from the outward man to the inward man because there is an increasing alignment as both are bound by the same universal. We must allow the norms of God in values and knowing to bind the inward man as well as the outward man, so that there is less and less discrepancy between the inward man and the outward man.

Unhappily, we will not perfectly keep God's norm more in the internal world of thought than we do externally, and even (in a fallen world) perhaps not as much. But with God's norms of truth, morals, values, and knowing, we have tracks (or, perhaps a better analogy, a North Star) which give unity to the internal and external world. God's norms not only give unity, but they provide a bridge between these two worlds. This applies both for ourselves, and then to get down inside each other. When we step from the external to the internal world of thought, we are not on a sea without a shore either in regard to ourselves or in regard to the woman or the man who stands before us.

For those who are walking through the swamps of this present generation, this is beauty. As this is understood, suddenly the inward man is no longer autonomous and there is a bringing together of the particulars about the inward man and the outward man under the same universal, and with this unity, thank God, we can really begin to get inside each other.

This, too, ought to be part of salvation, of the continuing work of Christ in the Christian's life. It is the loss of this that has deprived this poor generation of any real human communication. Men and women who sleep together for years, over and over again, are shut off from each other, because there is no universal that binds the inward particulars and the outward particulars. But to the Christian there is. As we grow spiritually and bring the inward particulars of the thought world—meaning, values, knowledge, and morals—under the norms of God, to that extent gradually what we seem to be outwardly increasingly conforms to what we are inwardly, so that we can really know each other.

I have spoken of myself looking outward and of other people looking at me. Now, the third result of the Christian view of epistemology is this: reality and imagination. In a way, this is the most important of the three. We were considering in an earlier chapter the modern view of epistemology, where modern man has no distinction between reality and fantasy. Now I am talking about the reverse side of that for the Christian. I live in a thought world which is filled with creativity; inside my head there is creative imagination. Why? Because God, who is the Creator, has made me in his own image, I can go out in imagination beyond the stars. This is true not only for the Christian, but for every man. Every man is made in the image of God; therefore, no man in his imagination is confined to his own body. Going out in our imagination, we can change something of the form of the universe as a result of our thought world—in our painting, in our poetry, or as an engineer, or a gardener. Is that not wonderful? It is not just a matter of photography, like Antonioni's *Blowup*—click, click, click. I am there, and I am able to impose the results of my imagination on the external world.

But notice this. Being a Christian and knowing that God has made the external world, there is no confusion for me between that which is imaginary and that which is real. The Christian is free; free to fly, because he is not confused between his fantasy and the reality which God has made. So we are not inwardly confused. We are free to say, "This is imagination." Is it not marvelous to be a painter and make things a little different from nature—not just to "photograph" nature but to make things a little different? Is it not wonderful to be made in the image of God and be able to use our creativity in this way? But although this is true, as a Christian I have the epistemology that enables me not to get confused between what I think and what is objectively real. The modern generation does not have this, and this is the reason why some youngsters are all torn up in these areas. But Christians should not be torn up here.

Thus the Christian may have fantasy and imagination without being threatened. Modern man cannot have daydreams and fantasy without being threatened. The Christian should be the person who is alive, whose imagination absolutely boils, which moves, which produces something a bit different from God's world because God made us to be creative.

In conclusion, we see three interrelated results of the Christian's view of epistemology, not separate but interwoven: first, as I look out to the external world, to the world of relationships, in the subject-object relationship; second, as other people look to me and I look to other people—as I want to know and understand another person; and third, to the internal world of my thoughts, fantasies, and imaginations. I look outward and I understand why there is a subject-object relationship. I look at another man, a non-Christian, and I know he is made in the image of God. As Christians allow the norms of Scripture more and more to bring together the inward and the outward man, we can know each other in greater and greater beauty and greater and greater depth. And, because he is not threatened by the difference between reality and fantasy, the Christian should be the man with the flaming imagination and the beauty of creativity. All of these things are ours. The modern alienation in the area of epistemology can make each of these three areas literally into a thing of black horror. The loss of the reality of the subject-object relationship; the impossibility of people getting to know each other; and the awful nightmare of the confusion between reality and fantasy: modern epistemology makes each of these three things into a terror. But under the unity of the apex of the infinite-personal God, in all of these areas we can have meaning, we can have reality, and we can have beauty. It is truth, but also beauty.

Because man revolted against God and tried to stand autonomous, the great alienation is in the area of man's separation from God. When that happened, then everything else went. This autonomy is carried over into the very basic area of epistemology, of knowing, so that man is not only divided from other men in the area of knowing, he is divided from himself. If there are no common categories between the internal fantasy and the external world, man is divided and feels alienated from himself. He has no universals to cover the particulars in his own life. He is one thing inside and another thing outside. Then he begins to scream, "Who am I?" Does that sound familiar to any of you who do Christian work today? At L'Abri we have youngsters come from the ends of the earth and say, "I have come to try to find out who I am." It is not just some psychological thing, as we usually think of psychological. It is basically epistemological. Man's attempted autonomy has robbed him of any certain reality. He has nothing to be sure of when his imagination soars beyond the stars if there is nothing to make a distinction between reality and fantasy. But on the basis of the Christian epistemology, this confusion is ended, the alienation is healed. This is the heart of the problem of knowing, and it is not solved until our knowledge fits under the apex of the infinite-personal, Triune God who is there, and who is not silent. When it does, and only when it does, there simply is no problem in the area of epistemology.

Appendices

Is Propositional
1 Revelation
Nonsense?

*T*here are two ways to consider the question of propositional revelation and infallibility. The first is through consideration of the presuppositions involved; and the second is through consideration of the detailed problems. This appendix will deal with the first. Until the first is in place, the second cannot be sensibly pursued.

To modern man, and much modern theology, the concept of propositional revelation and of the historic Christian view of infallibility is not so much mistaken as meaningless. It is so in the same way, and for the same basic reasons, that to most modern men and most modern theology the concept of sin and guilt, in any real moral sense, is meaningless. But, of course, one must ask if their presupposition is the proper and adequate one.

The Christian presupposition is that there was a personal beginning to all things— someone has been there and made all the rest.

This someone would have to be big enough and this means being infinite. One still has the question of the personal-infinite someone always having been there; but if this were the case the other problems would no longer exist. *And anyway, everyone has to explain the fact that the universe and he, the individual, exist; thus, something has "been there"!*

Now if this personal-infinite someone always having been there is the case, everything else would be limited in contrast to his own enough-ness, or infinite-ness. But just suppose that he made something limited, but on his own wave-length—let's say in his own image—then one would have both an infinite, non-created Personal and a limited, created personal. On this presupposition, the personality of the limited, created personal would be explained. On this same presupposition, why could not the non-created Personal communicate to the created personal if he wished? Of course, if the infinite, uncreated Personal communicated to the finite, created personal, he would not exhaust himself in his communication; but two things are clear here:

1. Even communication between one created person and another is not exhaustive; but that does not mean that for that reason it is not true. Thus, the problem of communication from the uncreated Personal to the created personal would *not* have to be of a qualitatively different order from the communication between one created personal being and another. It would not be exhaustive, but that would not make it untrue, any more than for the created-person to created-person communication to be untrue, unless the uncreated Personal were a liar or capricious.

2. If the uncreated Personal really cared for the created personal, it could not be thought unexpected for him to tell the created personal things of a propositional nature; otherwise, as a finite being, the created personal would have numerous things he could not know if he just

began with himself as a limited, finite reference point.

In such a case, there is no intrinsic reason why the uncreated Personal could communicate some vaguely true things, but could not communicate propositional truth concerning the world surrounding the created personal—for fun, let's call that science. Or why he could not communicate propositional truth to the created personal concerning the sequence that followed the uncreated Personal's making everything he made—let's call that history. There is no reason we could think of why he could not truly communicate these two types of propositional things. The communication would not be exhaustive, but could we think of any reason why it would not be true?

The above is, of course, what the Bible claims for itself in regard to propositional revelation.

If the uncreated Personal wished to give these communications through individual created personalities in such a way that they would write, in their own individual style, etc., the exact things the uncreated Personal wanted them to write in the areas of religious truth and things of the cosmos and history—then by this time it is pretty hard to make an absolute and say that he could not or would not. And this, of course, is the Bible's claim concerning inspiration.

Within this framework, why would it be unthinkable that the non-created Personal should communicate with the created personal in verbalized form, if the non-created Personal made the created personal a language-communicating being? And we are (even if we do not know why) language-communicating beings. There is only one reason to rule out as unthinkable the fact that Jesus gave a propositional communication to Saul in verbalized form in the Hebrew language, using normal words and syntax (Acts 26:14), or that God did so to the Jews at Sinai: that is, to have accepted the other set of presuppositions—even if, by using religious terminology, one obscures that one has accepted the naturalistic presuppositions. Now one may obscure what one has done in accepting naturalistic presuppositions by using religious terminology and saying or implying: "Jesus (without in this case having any way to know what that really is) gave to Saul some form of a first-order, non-contentful experience, in which the words used in the biblical text to express this inexpressible are just words which reflect views of life, history, and the cosmos which were then current." If one does this, however, one is left with a faith which is equivalent to saying, "I believe. . ." without ever finishing, or being able to finish, the sentence—or even knowing if a definite or an indefinite article comes next in the sentence.

Further, if the non-created Personal placed the communication he gave man in a book of history, why would it then be unlikely that the non-created Personal would communicate truly concerning the space-time history in that book? How strange that if the non-created Personal is not a liar or capricious, he should give "religious truth" in a book in which the whole structural framework, implicity and explicitly, is historic, and yet that history be false or confused. Surely, except on the preconceived presupposition that that book can only be "man feeling upward" within the framework of the uniformity of natural causes, such an idea would be peculiar beyond measure. This is especially so, as the book itself gives no indication of two levels; it gives no indication of a "religious truth" out of contact with the history in the book. It repeatedly appeals to the history as open to verification as a proof of the truth of what is given; and it gives no indication of the enveloping space-time history being only so much error-conditioned incrustation.

Why could not the non-created Personal teach the created personal truly on that level of knowledge which is the basis of so much of that which we know on the created personal level: namely, one who knows, telling one who does not know—not exhaustively, yet truly? Surely this is how we have our knowledge from other created personal sources. Further, why could not the non-created Personal also tell about himself truly (though not exhaustively)— unless we have already accepted the presupposition that that which is the "non-created" must be the "philosophic other." If we begin with a non-created Personal creating man in his own image, what rules out the statement of the Westminster Larger Catechism that God made known to us, through the Scripture, what God is? Is there any reason why the non-created Personal could not so tell us truly about himself, though not exhaustively?

By this stage, two things should be obvious: first, that from the presupposition that all things started from mass or energy, the idea of either revelation or infallibility is unthinkable; and second, that from the presupposition of a personal beginning, these ideas are not unthinkable or nonsense at all. The reasonableness of the matter thus rests totally on which way one begins, that is, on which presupposition one adopts at the outset.

If one starts with the impersonal everything, then the question naturally has nothing to do with even the possibility of an uncreated Personal communicating to a created personal; that, from the premise, is nonsense. Yet if one does begin with a non-personal everything, there is a question that now really shouts: Is not man-to-man communication equally nonsense?

With this presupposition no one has discovered a way to find meaning either in man's speaking to man or in man's hearing, except through an act of faith against his whole basic presuppositional structure. Worse yet, for those who hold this other presupposition, the little men (I and the others) are not content to think that they do not speak meaningfully; and everything in experience convinces us that the others hear truly, though not exhaustively.

By this time, is this not something like a Francis Bacon painting? One must scream—but the whole situation is a lostness and a damnation, including the scream.

Well now, in the light of this total confusion to which the other presupposition (the impersonal + time + chance) leads us, the presupposition of a personal beginning is worth another very careful look. If everything did begin with that uncreated Personal beginning, then neither communication from the created personal to the created personal, nor from the non-created Personal to the created personal is unthinkable. Nor is it even intrinsically unlikely.

The importance of all this is that most people today (including some who still call themselves evangelical) who have given up the historical and biblical concept of revelation and infallibility have not done so because of the consideration of detailed problems objectively approached, but because they have accepted, either in analyzed fashion or blindly, the other set of presuppositions. Often they have done this by means of injection, without realizing what has happened to them.

Having accepted the other presupposition against the evidence of true, though not exhaustive, man-to-man communication, I wonder what would make them listen? It is strange to communicate truly the concept that one rejects the concept of a non-created Personal "being there," when there is no way then to know the how, why, or what of communication with my own kind. And the strangeness continues then to say that it is unreasonable *per se* to consider the fact of the non-created Personal being there, when that would explain the how, why, and what of the communication I do have with my own kind!

Having come to this point we are in a position to consider the detailed problems. But the historic view of the Bible and of the church about revelation and infallibility is no longer nonsense *per se;* and even most of the detailed problems look very different once the nonsense connotation is dealt with.

2 "Faith" Versus Faith

One must analyze the word *faith* and see that it can mean two completely opposite things.

Suppose we are climbing in the Alps and are very high on the bare rock and suddenly the fog shuts down. The guide turns to us and says that the ice is forming and that there is no hope; before morning we will all freeze to death here on the shoulder of the mountain. Simply to keep warm, the guide keeps us moving in the dense fog further out on the shoulder until none of us have any idea where we are. After an hour or so, someone says to the guide: "Suppose I dropped and hit a ledge ten feet down in the fog. What would happen then?" The guide would say that you might make it till the morning and thus live. So, with absolutely no knowledge or any reason to support his action, one of the group hangs and drops into the fog. This would be one kind of faith, a leap of faith.

Suppose, however, after we have worked out on the shoulder in the midst of the fog and the growing ice on the rock, we had stopped and we heard a voice which said: "You cannot see me, but I know exactly where you are from your voices. I am on another ridge. I have lived in these mountains, man and boy, for over sixty years and I know every foot of them. I assure you that ten feet below you there is a ledge. If you hang and drop, you can make it through the night and I will get you in the morning."

I would not hang and drop at once, but would ask questions to try to ascertain if the man knew what he was talking about and if he was not my enemy. In the Alps, for example, I would ask him his name. If the name he gave me was the name of a family from that part of the mountains, it would count a great deal to me. In the Swiss Alps there are certain family names that indicate mountain families of that area. For example, in the area of the Alps where I live, Avanthey would be such a name. In my desperate situation, even though time would be running out, I would ask him what to me would be the sufficient questions, and when I became convinced by his answers, then I would hang and drop.

This is faith, but obviously it has no relationship to the first instance. As a matter of fact, if one of these is called faith, the other should not be designated by the same word symbol. The historic Christian faith is not a leap of faith in the post-Kierkegaardian sense because "he is not silent," and I am invited to ask the sufficient questions in regard to details but also in regard to the existence of the universe and its complexity and in regard to the existence of man. I am invited to ask the sufficient questions and then believe him and bow before him metaphysically in knowing that I exist because he made man, and bow before him morally as needing his provision for me in the substitutionary, propitiatory death of Christ.